THINKING on DEFENSE

The art of vi D0870490 *dge*

Jim Priebe

MASTER POINT PRESS
TORONTO

Master Point Press
331 Douglas Ave.
Toronto, Ontario, Canada
M5M 1H2

(416) 781-0351
www.masterpointpress.com

Canadian Cataloguing in Publication Data

Priebe, James A.
Thinking on defense

ISBN 1-894154-37-1

I. Contract bridge —Defensive play I. Title.

GV 1282. 42. P75 2001   795.41'53   C2001-901296-9

Cover and Interior design: Olena S. Sullivan
Editor: Ray Lee
Interior format and copyediting: Deanna Bourassa

Printed and bound in Canada by Webcom Limited

1 2 3 4 5 6 7   07 06 05 04 03 02 01

FOREWORD

Zia, in his modern classic, *Bridge My Way,* verbalized something that every good player knows instinctively — when he's in his best form (Zia's Heat One), everything comes easily to him. He "knows everything" without having to delve too deeply into the clues. He plays crisply and confidently and invariably does the right thing.

The problem, of course, is that Heat One never lasts. For even the best players in the world, the game is usually work. Hard work. In no facet of the game is this more apparent than in defense, which requires taking into consideration not only your personal a priori analysis of the layout but also an evaluation of the cards that both your partner and declarer have played or might have played with particular holdings. Add to this exercise an assessment of the abilities and current intensity of those players and an appreciation of the form of scoring and perhaps even the state of the match and it becomes clear that mastering the art of defense is probably impossible. The best we can do is to teach ourselves to think clearly, to eliminate extraneous information and dead ends, and to stay focused on the true objective of each deal.

When it comes to objectives, IMPs and Rubber Bridge are much easier games than Matchpoints. The defenders go all out to defeat the contract. The complexities and nuances of Matchpoint defense make this form of scoring a completely different game. Normal versus abnormal contracts, sacrifices, the extra 10 or 20 points for choosing one strain over another, determining whether the defense should protect its result or go all out to try to improve it — each of these subjects could fill a few chapters of a complete book on defense, a tome that should properly run to a thousand pages.

Jim Priebe's book on defense will not explore all of these avenues. Instead, it will focus on clarity of thought, in particular on the concept of visualization, the process of picturing several possible hands for declarer consistent with all the information available to the defender at the critical juncture in the play (there may be several). The art — and it is an art — lies in choosing the play that caters to the most likely or several of the most likely layouts consistent with the objectives of the defenders in each case.

Why the special interest in defense? In analyzing his own defensive lapses, Jim felt that at the bottom of most of them was a failure to sift through alternatives, to jump too quickly to a conclusion, and to base his defensive play on the first reasonable hand to come to mind. Although his passion for the game was always strong, Jim never had the time he would have liked to devote to the game until he retired from business a few years ago.

Borrowing an idea from his business training, Jim concluded that "visualizing" alternatives and analyzing them before committing to a course of action would inevitably improve his own play immeasurably. He soon found that adopting this approach and sticking to it made a significant difference and led him to write this book with the hope that he can help others willing to invest in a little hard work.

First books by unknown authors are often unappreciated by the bridge community, but it would be a mistake to pass this one up. Invest some time and effort and read what Jim has to say. Doing so will improve not only your defense and your partner's but will also elevate your appreciation and respect for the game to a level you may have forgotten or might not yet have considered.

Erik Kokish
Toronto, August, 2001

Contents

To my wife Joan
a wonderful help in preparing this manuscript
and a great partner in every way.

INTRODUCTION

Most players are aware that they throw away

noticeably more tricks per relevant deal on defense

than they do on offense.

Jeff Rubens, **The Bridge World**

This book is intended for players who have achieved some success at their current level of bridge competition, whatever that may be, and are keen to play and win at a higher level. Thus, its purpose is to help ambitious players become strong defenders.

The objective of the defending side, in general, is to take as many tricks as possible. More specifically, a defender's objectives are:

- To defeat the opponents' voluntarily bid contracts, whether they are in a partscore, game or slam.

- To extract the maximum penalty when the opponents are overboard, whether you have doubled them or not.

- To allow as few overtricks as possible.

The first two are of overwhelming importance in IMP games. All three apply at matchpoints, and that is what makes defense at matchpoints so delightfully complex. This book will mainly focus on the first objective, that is, on setting the contract. This is where bushels of IMPs and matchpoints are squandered and where a little extra work on the part of the defenders will show its biggest payoff. Overtricks and maximum undertricks will be treated, then, as important but secondary issues.

I am going to introduce you to the idea of *visualization*, which involves forming a mental picture of a small number of possible hands for declarer. This concept is a unifying thread which weaves its way through the book and strengthens your application of other defensive fundamentals. If you can master even a part of the visualization process, you will see an immediate improvement in your results.

Chapter 1 discusses why defense is so important in terms of the matchpoint percentage or IMPs at stake. In it, I shall attempt to persuade you that undertaking the work involved in the rest of this book will have some very real payback for you in terms of your own scores.

Chapter 2 introduces the subject of visualization, explains what it is, and shows how to go about it. The process described in Chapter 2 works its way through all of the other chapters.

Chapters 3, 4 and 5 detail the fundamental skills which a good defender needs at his fingertips at all times:

- agreements with partner on opening leads and signals

- counting

- understanding defensive tactics

- recognizing and combating what declarer is doing.

Finally, Chapter 6 contains forty problems which will provide you with opportunities to practice the concepts. These problems are real-life examples, many of them from World Championship competition, where you will find that applying the visualization process will enable you to improve on the original result at the table. Once you've reached this stage, you'll find that your own results as a defender will get better too.

Why Bother?

A good defensive player is always

a winner over the long haul.

Eddie Kantar, **Defensive Bridge Play**

Defense is an insidious part of the game of bridge. On some days, you may find that you encounter no special challenge in the hands you defend. Perhaps your partner had all the critical decisions, or maybe on these occasions your routine defensive methods (leads and signals) covered all the problem hands nicely. Other times, you find that you have doubled a partscore on Board 1, with four percent of a matchpoint session's work resting on your shoulders alone (or 18 IMPs if you are playing a team game — gain 6 IMPs by setting the contract, or lose 12 if it makes). Worse still, the key play may ambush you at Trick 1 instead of presenting itself in a leisurely way at Trick 12, when you have plenty of information.

Most experts agree, too, that defense is the toughest part of the game of bridge. When players gather after a session one seldom hears defense discussed. It is too hard! It is rare that there are quick and easy answers to defensive problems. And defense is often complex. When you say, 'I played the king because it loses only when partner had jack-ten-eight, and if he had jack-ten-seven or worse, it couldn't cost,' you find your friends looking away and changing the subject. In any case, improving players generally are advised that bidding is the most important skill to develop, and they focus on learning the latest conventions and the laws of this and that. A large number become very competent declarers indeed, since that is a proficiency that is easy to study alone. The majority of bridge players, however, completely neglect their development as defenders.

Even among those who want to improve as defenders, few players realize their potential; they do not understand how to go about developing their defensive skills. Of course, they will spend much time agreeing on a system of opening leads, and they probably hold earnest discussions on what signaling system to use. Many players can tell you the main tactics available to a defender, such as preventing a ruff or attacking declarer's communications. A few become careful counters of points and distribution, and use this information when making their plays. An even smaller group tries to fathom what declarer is doing and then counter his tactics. All these are important weapons in the arsenal of a good defensive player. Necessary, even vital, but not sufficient, I say.

As a defender, you do not know your side's exact assets, and even though you grasp defender's tactics and count meticulously, unless you go through a process of visualization (which involves opening your mind to several possibilities instead of focussing on just one) you will often overlook the right play. The hardest part, no doubt, but the crucial element in becoming a top defensive player, lies in developing the ability to visualize possible hands around the table, sorting out which ones are most likely, and which, if any, the defense can do something about.

We have all heard that bidding is all-important and that defense rarely swings matches in the finals of World Championship or National team play. (There are notable exceptions to this, including the 1982 World Championship, the spectacular last board of the 2000 Vanderbilt, and Board 116 of the 2000 ITT semifinal.) Why, then, should anyone bother working to improve their defensive ability if few matches are swung on defense?

First, you should remember that only the very best players get to play in the finals of National and World Championships, and you can be sure that these players have invested the time and the effort necessary to become top defenders. At every level except the finals, many IMPs change hands as a result of defensive play. In the course of studying several hundred deals in top-level play, I found a big difference between results in the early stages of a competition and those in the finals and semifinals. In the World Championship Round Robin matches I looked at, 1200 IMPs were won and lost, the cause being split almost evenly between bidding and card play. Of the 600 IMPs swung in card play, declarer play and defense were again about equal, so defense accounted for one quarter of the IMPs that changed hands. In the finals, however, bidding accounted for eighty percent of the swings, with only twenty percent coming from play and defense. Why? Because the finalists had driven themselves to high standards of defensive capability.

Outside of a handful of the very top bridge stars, there are great opportunities for players to improve their defensive performance, whether at IMPs or matchpoints, in local club games or national events, playing kitchen bridge or in high-stakes rubber games. Believe me, the potential gain is well worth the pain.

WHAT'S AT STAKE AT IMPS?

First and foremost at IMPs, the object of the defense is to set the contract. Sure, there have been plenty of matches tied and decided in overtime, and others won by an IMP or two, but they are a small percentage of the total. Tough players focus on the set.

The odds favor aggressive defenders by a significant margin. In lowly partscore contracts, you gain 4 IMPs setting a non-vulnerable partscore made by your teammates, and 5 IMPs setting a vulnerable contract made at the other table. Defending against game contracts, if you set a contract which is made by your teammates, you gain 10 IMPs (12 IMPs vulnerable). Slam defenses are even more lucrative. Setting a small slam made at the other table yields 14 IMPs (16 IMPs vulnerable).

There are two exceptions to this line of thinking. First, in defending many hands, you soon realize that there is no possibility of setting the contract. You have no reason in these cases to make declarer a gift of overtricks in a vain attempt to achieve the impossible. The job of the defenders changes to 'do everything possible to minimize overtricks.'

The second case involves play in Swiss team events. On the thirty-point victory point scale that is often used, a 1-IMP win gives you a margin of 18-12, and a 2-IMP win results in a 19-11 tally. The victory points in close matches are levered excessively in favor of the winners. Thus you should never lose focus on those potentially important overtricks. They can become especially important when one of these short matches involves some routine partscores and easy games.

IMP scoring brings with it another danger, a kind of double jeopardy, even though no-one expects to be punished twice for the same offense. This happens whenever an aggressive contract is reached at one table and not at the other. Now poor defensive play can be magnified into an enormous swing. Defenders beware!

Similarly, think about the perils of doubled partscores. If you concede 530 and partners are plus 110, you score minus 9 IMPs. When you find a set on a doubled hand and your teammates make a plus score, you gain 5 IMPs, so the total swing hanging on your defensive play is 14 IMPs (not vulnerable) or 19 IMPs (vulnerable).

IMP players tend to be very aggressive in bidding games, especially when vulnerable. Suppose you are selected to play against the wild pair on an opposing team because of your defensive acumen. It helps to understand the mathematics. When they bid a bad game while your teammates are in a partscore, and you let them make it, you score up minus 7 instead of plus 5 (12 IMPs not vulnerable) or minus 10 instead of plus 6 (16 IMPs vulnerable).

Then there are the slams. I don't bid as many silly slams as I used to (increased wisdom has to be some compensation for advancing years) but sometimes opponents do. When you defend, you score minus 11 IMPs if they make, versus plus 11 if you set them. When partners bid sanely or conservatively, this computes to 22 IMPs not vulnerable (25 IMPs vulnerable). That's more than enough to decide many matches.

WHAT'S AT STAKE AT MATCHPOINTS?

Bidding at matchpoints is a touch more conservative, with many players opting for a plus score instead of a big gain. At least, that's the
theory. However, the theory doesn't seem to hold in the games I play in!
I get to defend as many aggressive contracts at matchpoints as anywhere
else. When you add in the factors of lively competitive partscore auc-
tions and more doubled partscores, it is easy to see how important
defense is to matchpoint players.

The math is more difficult at matchpoints than at IMPs just because
there is more guesswork. Let's try anyway. When do you go for a set?

- If the opponents are in a doubled or unusual contract and you're
  dead (in terms of your matchpoint score) if they make it.

- If partner has made a good lead and has created an opportunity
  that may not be available at all tables.

- If you need a good board because of your estimated position in
  the event.

- Any time a line of defense to set a contract is consistent with
  available information.

Is any math possible? I looked over some data from a National Life
Master Pairs, with a top of 100. The data shows huge variance, but it is
still possible to draw some general conclusions. The value of an overtrick averaged 25 matchpoints. The value of setting a game or partscore
contract versus allowing it to make was 50 matchpoints. A slam that
could be set generally accounted for 90% of the matchpoints on a board.
I looked over several years of hands from the Epson and Alcatel pairs
contests, and found roughly the same percentages (also with large variance).

In the context of a 26-board duplicate game, each hand counts for
just under 4% of a session's potential score. Setting a contract can jump
your score 2%, while preventing an overtrick will inch you up 1%. Solid
defense can make the difference between having your scores languish in
the 50% bracket and moving frequently into the magic sixties.

Is there such a thing as double jeopardy at matchpoints? Impossible,
you might say. But consider the case where you are contending in a pairs
event, and you sit down to play two boards against the pair who are leading the field with sixty-five percent while you are cruising at sixty. Each
of the two boards is worth four percent in the session. Let us say you get

two defensive opportunities, and capitalize on them to gain two clear tops. You knock this pair down to sixty percent, and raise your score to sixty-three percent, putting you in a great position to win*. Of course at matchpoints, unless there is barometer scoring, such as one finds in ACBL internet tournaments, you may not know exactly how you are doing nor where your current opposition stands. Nevertheless, you can often form a general idea of the importance of the boards against each opposing pair before you play them, and the main point remains: just as is the case for baseball, football and hockey teams, defense can win championships.

As you will see after the next chapter, the better your visualization, the more accurately you can estimate the risk/reward from an aggressive line of defense. This is especially important at matchpoints.

---

* Footnote for the numerically skeptical
OPPONENTS: 24 boards at 65% plus 2 boards at 0% equals 26 boards at 60%
THE GOOD GUYS: 24 boards at 60% plus 2 boards at 100% equals 26 boards at 63.08%

CHAPTER 2

Thinking on Defense

The bridge player is investigating the present realities at all stages of his task; asking himself, in the light of the evidence, what cards lie in which positions. Then he acts on his findings, constructing, synthesizing in a small way.

Gerald Abrahams, **Brains in Bridge**

Visualization is a form of lateral thinking, the mental process of exploring multiple possibilities and approaches instead of pursuing a single approach. To a defender, exploring multiple possibilities means training yourself to construct and examine several potential declarer hands as you plan each defensive campaign. You sift through two, three or four alternative hands, and only then make your decision on what card to play. You are careful in the use of instinctive plays — these are the cliches of bridge, and are usually poison to defenders; for example:

- never lead trumps;

- always return partner's lead;

- third hand high;

- second hand low;

- lead through strength, up to weakness.

These statements have value for whist and euchre players, and for beginning bridge players. *They have no place in the arsenal of an aspiring defensive expert.* You need a specific reason for every card that you play (which may just be hope in some cases!) based on your visualization of declarer's hand.

ACQUIRING VISUALIZATION SKILLS

Visualizing unseen hands means thinking through alternatives. As a good defender, you mentally construct three or four possible hands, select one or two where a play is critical, and only then play your card. During a session of twenty-six boards you can expect to encounter two or three difficult defensive problems. Each of these hands will have a turning point where the play that you choose will be the sole factor determining the result. At that defensive turning point, the bidding is history, the opening lead has done its damage, declarer may have fired his best shot, and the defense is in charge. Getting those critical hands right each session will improve your matchpoint percentages markedly and make you a sought-after teammate for IMP matches.

On defense, you compile information from the bidding, from partner's lead and signals, and from declarer's tactics. As you ponder what you should play, you will probably not know your side's exact assets. In piecing together a hand for declarer (and thus for partner) you must engage in a certain amount of guesswork. While a good defender frequently guesses correctly, it is easy to fall into the trap of assigning one specific hand to declarer and basing your whole defense on that hand. Later, when the specific layout is clear, you may find that you have missed the mark.

When you pause to visualize, you need to form a mental picture of a range of possibilities instead of just one possible hand. You want the range to be small enough so that you can get your mind around it, but broad enough so that you do not overlook any hand that is reasonably possible for declarer. Even at an early stage of a hand there is useful information to help define the range. Notrump bids, five-card majors, and any number of special conventions are revealing. Leads, signals, and the first few tricks all add vital data. The goal of the visualization process is to make sure that you, the defender, like a good strategist in business, war or politics, consider the alternatives broadly enough to make a good decision.

With a few possible hands for declarer in mind, then, you set about the task of eliminating those where your task is hopeless. For example, if a hand does not jibe with information from partner's lead and signals, move on. If your count of points and distribution tells you that a hand is impossible, ignore it. Playing IMPs, drop from further consideration any hand that means the contract cannot be set.

When do you pause and carry out your visualization? Start before the first trick has been turned over. Routine hands look after themselves; only difficult hands require an investment of significant mental effort. On these difficult hands, the defender must start early and be ready for the turning point. If you are not ready when the time comes, your hesitation itself may cost the contract.

STEP BY STEP

You may be asking yourself, 'Are there any shortcuts in the visualization process? Must I go through this lengthy analysis on every hand I play?' This depends on where you are in your development as a defensive player. Many hands can be analyzed with reference to one suit only, or one or two key suits. You can see clearly that partner needs a specific holding to give you any chance of a good result: at IMPs, setting the contract, or at matchpoints, taking the maximum number of tricks. The more experienced you are, the easier and shorter the visualization process becomes. Let us follow these themes through the defense of a single hand; then, change the hand and see how the approach changes.

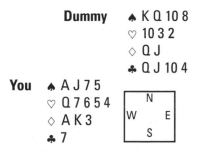

Dummy ♠ K Q 10 8
♡ 10 3 2
◇ Q J
♣ Q J 10 4

You ♠ A J 7 5
♡ Q 7 6 5 4
◇ A K 3
♣ 7

Your opponents settle in 3NT after South opens a 15-17 notrump and North's Stayman enquiry reveals that he has no four-card major. Your heart lead is won by declarer's jack. Quick, what are you going to do when declarer immediately plays a low spade? You, as West, must be ready when declarer's spade hits the table. All of your thinking must be done before you turn over the first trick.

Ducking even one spade is dangerous. Declarer is marked with all the outstanding high cards (the ace, king, jack of hearts and the ace, king of clubs). If declarer has five clubs, one spade trick will let him waltz away with his contract. You need to find partner with some diamond holding such as 109xx, 10xxxx, or xxxxxx; any of those holdings produces five, six or seven tricks for the defense. It takes little or no analysis to see that rising with the ace of spades and playing diamonds is the right defense.

Remove the jack of spades from your hand and you have a slightly different problem after the same play to Trick 1:

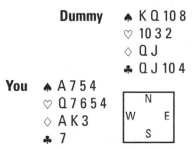

Dummy ♠ K Q 10 8
♡ 10 3 2
◇ Q J
♣ Q J 10 4

You ♠ A 7 5 4
♡ Q 7 6 5 4
◇ A K 3
♣ 7

Again, declarer surely has the ace and king of clubs, and the ace, king, and jack of hearts. The important unknown factors here are the number of clubs declarer holds and the locations of the ten of diamonds and the jack of spades. We can construct possible hands around the table, and then analyze them to see where they lead the defense.

VARIATION 1

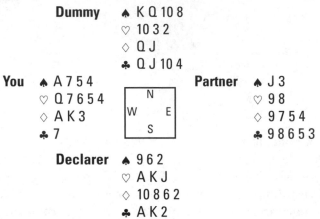

	Dummy	♠ K Q 10 8
		♡ 10 3 2
		◇ Q J
		♣ Q J 10 4

You ♠ A 7 5 4   **Partner** ♠ J 3
     ♡ Q 7 6 5 4   ♡ 9 8
     ◇ A K 3   ◇ 9 7 5 4
     ♣ 7   ♣ 9 8 6 5 3

Declarer ♠ 9 6 2
            ♡ A K J
            ◇ 10 8 6 2
            ♣ A K 2

In this variation, if you win the first spade and play three rounds of diamonds, declarer has all his work done for him, and makes ten tricks. This is not a great issue at IMPs, but at matchpoints the play delivers a below-average result for the defense. Declarer can achieve this result himself by guessing the spade position, but ducking the spade gives the defense hope for four tricks.

VARIATION 2

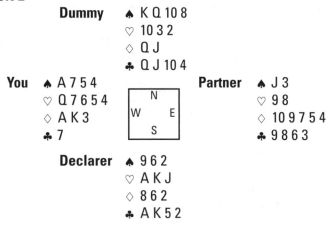

	Dummy	♠ K Q 10 8
		♡ 10 3 2
		◇ Q J
		♣ Q J 10 4

You ♠ A 7 5 4   **Partner** ♠ J 3
     ♡ Q 7 6 5 4   ♡ 9 8
     ◇ A K 3   ◇ 10 9 7 5 4
     ♣ 7   ♣ 9 8 6 3

Declarer ♠ 9 6 2
            ♡ A K J
            ◇ 8 6 2
            ♣ A K 5 2

Here, the defense gets two chances, because declarer needs two spade tricks for his contract. If you duck the second spade, declarer is home. He will surely play you for the ace of spades because he cannot afford to lose the lead. If you win either the first or second spade, the defense can take six tricks.

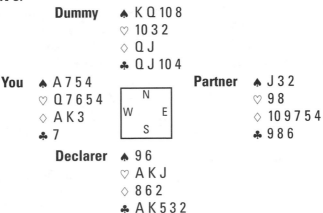

```
                Dummy     ♠ K Q 10 8
                          ♡ 10 3 2
                          ◇ Q J
                          ♣ Q J 10 4
     You  ♠ A 7 5 4              Partner  ♠ J 3 2
          ♡ Q 7 6 5 4                     ♡ 9 8
          ◇ A K 3                         ◇ 10 9 7 5 4
          ♣ 7                             ♣ 9 8 6
              Declarer    ♠ 9 6
                          ♡ A K J
                          ◇ 8 6 2
                          ♣ A K 5 3 2
```

Now ducking one spade is a disaster because that is declarer's ninth trick. You must win the ace of spades the first time spades are led, and play diamonds.

We could go on, but three examples are plenty at this stage. In all three cases we constructed, it costs nothing to win the ace of spades at IMPs, while ducking can never gain. At matchpoints, the choice of play is perhaps not as clear. If we change your diamond holding to A32 or K32, the same idea is valid. You can tell that declarer either has solid clubs or is traveling to dummy to finesse against partner's club king, a play that will bring good news. If declarer lacks the king of clubs, he surely has a diamond honor. Let us look at this new variation to see what we can learn.

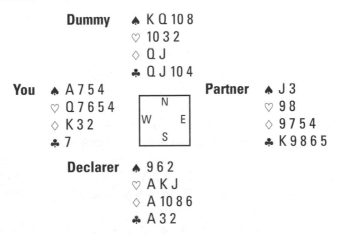

```
                Dummy     ♠ K Q 10 8
                          ♡ 10 3 2
                          ◇ Q J
                          ♣ Q J 10 4
     You  ♠ A 7 5 4              Partner  ♠ J 3
          ♡ Q 7 6 5 4                     ♡ 9 8
          ◇ K 3 2                         ◇ 9 7 5 4
          ♣ 7                             ♣ K 9 8 6 5
              Declarer    ♠ 9 6 2
                          ♡ A K J
                          ◇ A 10 8 6
                          ♣ A 3 2
```

Rising with the ace of spades and shifting to a diamond will lead to declarer making five notrump. He could do this himself, but needs to guess the spade position. If your diamonds were ◇A32, the same result would ensue.

From this point on, instead of showing variations with a diagram of all four hands, I will show only your hand and dummy, to define the problem. Then I will suggest two or more possible hands for declarer. The constructed hands will take into account the information available to the defenders from the bidding and from partner's and declarer's play to date. This mimics the real-life process of visualization that I am recommending. The same approach is used throughout the other example and problem hands in the book.

With a diamond holding of K103 or A103, the defense is less certain. Suppose this is the problem you see after your heart lead is again won by the jack, and declarer tables a low spade:

Dummy ♠ K Q 10 8
          ♡ 10 3 2
          ◊ Q J
          ♣ Q J 10 4

You ♠ A 7 5 4
     ♡ Q 7 6 5 4
     ◊ K 10 3
     ♣ 7

```
        N
    W       E
        S
```

You can consider three possible hands for declarer as you plan your defense.

Hand 1	**Hand 2**	**Hand 3**
♠ 9 6 2	♠ 9 6	♠ 9 6
♡ A K J	♡ A K J	♡ A K J
◊ 8 6 2	◊ A 8 6 2	◊ 8 6 2
♣ A K 5 3	♣ A 9 3 2	♣ A K 5 3 2

Against Hand 1, you have the luxury of two chances to set the hand: winning either the first or second spade and shifting to a diamond will give the defense six tricks. However, you must either shift to the king of diamonds and then play the ten, or shift to the ten, and with either of these leads you are bound to give partner a problem. Leading the ten suggests a poor diamond holding, perhaps with ace, queen to five hearts and the need for partner to lead a heart through declarer. Leading the diamond king and following with the ten will suggest a doubleton diamond.

However, if you lead the diamond ten, partner should work out that you cannot hold AQxxx in hearts because there would have been absolutely no rush to win the ace of spades and shift to a diamond. The only reason to rise with the ace of spades would be in the case where the defense must work on diamonds quickly. Partner can also reasonably reject a layout where a heart return is vital, such as the following declarer hand:

$$\spadesuit \; x\,x\,x \quad \heartsuit \; K\,J\,x \quad \diamond \; K\,x\,x \quad \clubsuit \; A\,K\,x\,x$$

While possible, this would be a sub-minimum hand for a 15-17 notrump bid.

If you switch to the king of diamonds and continue with the ten, partner will not have a problem if he holds A98x, A9xxx, or A8xxxx in the suit. He cannot go wrong either by ducking or by overtaking the ten. If partner has A8xx or A8xxx maximum damage has already been done, and declarer will be thankful of your help (Hand 4).

Against Hand 2, winning the ace of spades and shifting to a diamond allows declarer to make eleven tricks. He could do this himself of course, but your ducking the spade twice would give him a chance to misguess spades and hold himself to one overtrick.

Against Hand 3, you must win the ace of spades at your first opportunity and play diamonds; otherwise declarer will make his impossible game.

The contrast in thinking between IMPs and matchpoints stands out here. At IMPs, you have a very good chance of setting the contract if partner has a suitable diamond holding, and it is worth risking the loss of 1 IMP in pursuit of a 10- or 12-IMP gain (or avoidance of a similar loss if your counterpart at the other table finds the winning defense). At matchpoints, there is more to be said for ducking the spade twice because you preserve some chance for an above-average score. My recommendation for matchpoint players is that whenever you have a choice of two lines of defense which appear equally reasonable, you should adopt the route that leads to setting the contract. You get a bigger payoff (a near top for a set versus an above-average score for holding the contract tight).

THE PROCESS OF VISUALIZATION

This real-life example illustrates how a defender can use information from only the bidding to arrive at a winning play. This is the auction:

WEST	NORTH	EAST	SOUTH
You		*Partner*	
			1♣
1♠	dbl	3♠	4♡
4♠	pass	pass	5♣
pass	5♡	all pass	

You lead the king of spades and see this layout:

♠ 6 4
♡ A Q J 8
◇ 10 8 5 4
♣ Q J 10

♠ A K 10 8 5 2
♡ 5 4
◇ K 7
♣ 8 7 2

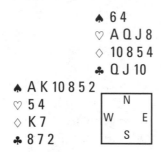

Partner plays the nine (a count card in this situation, showing an even number) and declarer the three. Your agreement with partner about the meaning of the three-spades bid is that it shows a constructive hand with four trumps but less than a limit raise. You review your chances and mentally synthesize a few possible hands for declarer. The outstanding high cards to account for here are the heart king, the ace and queen of diamonds, and the ace and king of clubs. Declarer no doubt has three or four of those cards. You know that declarer has four hearts and five or six clubs. These are the hands you imagine as you work out your play to Trick 2.

Hand 1	Hand 2	Hand 3	Hand 4
♠ 3	♠ 3	♠ 3	♠ 3
♡ 10 7 6 3	♡ K 10 6 3	♡ K 10 6 3	♡ 10 7 6 3
◇ A Q 3	◇ A Q 3	◇ Q J	◇ A 3
♣ A 9 6 5 4	♣ K 9 6 5 4	♣ A K 9 6 5 4	♣ A K 9 6 5 4

With Hand 1, declarer can take three heart tricks, five clubs, a diamond and a spade ruff in hand for ten tricks. The defense must be patient about their diamond trick because switching to a diamond now hands declarer his eleventh trick. Declarer's hand here is one that few players would open, let alone take to the five-level.

With Hand 2, declarer has four hearts, four clubs, a spade ruff and the ace of diamonds for ten tricks. A diamond switch again allows declarer to make an impossible game.

Defending against Hand 3, a diamond switch at Trick 2 allows the defense to cash the first three tricks, and against Hand 4, the diamond play lets partner cash a diamond when he wins the king of trumps.

Now we have a dilemma. On Hands 1 and 2, we must wait for a diamond trick, and on Hands 3 and 4, we must play a diamond immediately or we give up an unmakable game. What is the answer?

In this case, we should trust the opponents' bidding. The auction is much more credible when declarer holds six clubs, and offensive potential, than if he has only a five-card suit and reasonable defensive prospects. Therefore, the recommended play is the king of diamonds at Trick 2.

In fact, this was the actual deal (declarer had Hand 3 above):

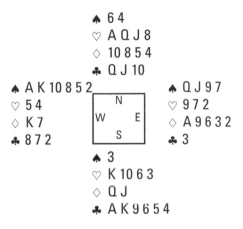

```
                ♠ 6 4
                ♡ A Q J 8
                ◇ 10 8 5 4
                ♣ Q J 10
♠ A K 10 8 5 2              ♠ Q J 9 7
♡ 5 4          ┌─────┐      ♡ 9 7 2
◇ K 7        W │  N  │ E    ◇ A 9 6 3 2
♣ 8 7 2        │  S  │      ♣ 3
               └─────┘
                ♠ 3
                ♡ K 10 6 3
                ◇ Q J
                ♣ A K 9 6 5 4
```

CONSTRUCTING POSSIBILITIES

The next three problems expand on the mental process of visualization. In each case, I am going to show two or more possible hands for declarer that are consistent with the bidding, with partner's lead and signals, and with the play so far. You will find that with some good hard mental effort, you become increasingly proficient at making the right decision.

Modern bidders understand that the better they can describe their hand patterns and high card values, the better their chances of getting to the right contract. They are right, but in the process, they provide help to the defenders. Such conventions as Flannery 2◇, mini-Roman 2◇ and two-suited two-bids provide precise information about distribution and high cards to the defense as well as to the offense. Five-card majors and narrow-ranged bids such as notrump calls provide inferences about strength and distribution that are useful to a defender trying to visualize possible declarer hands.

Here is such a case. You lead the jack of clubs against 3NT after the bidding has gone:

WEST	NORTH	EAST	SOUTH
You		*Partner*	
pass	pass	pass	1♡
dbl	1♠	pass	2NT
pass	3NT	all pass	

♠ J 9 6 4
♡ K Q
◇ Q 8 5 4
♣ 6 5 4

♠ A 10 8 2
♡ 5 4
◇ A J 7
♣ J 10 8 2

Partner follows with the three and declarer wins the queen. Declarer crosses to the king of hearts as partner follows low, and leads the four of spades to partner's three and his queen. You win the ace and pause to consider your defense. In order to illustrate the method, I will show six possible hands in this problem, more than a defender usually looks at.

The auction suggests that declarer is 5332, but you cannot yet rule out 5422 hands. Partner's attitude signal at Trick 1 tells you that declarer has nine points in clubs – half of his assets. When declarer shows the queen of spades, you can account for eleven of his eighteen or nineteen points. This leaves him with seven or eight other points. The three main outstanding high cards are the king of spades, the king of diamonds, and the ace of hearts. Partner has one of those cards, but at this point you do not know which one. These hands ought to bracket the possibilities.

Hand 1	Hand 2	Hand 3	Hand 4	Hand 5	Hand 6
♠ K Q	♠ K Q	♠ K Q	♠ K Q	♠ Q 3	♠ Q 3
♡ A J 7 6 3	♡ J 10 7 6 3	♡ J 9 7 6 3	♡ A 9 7 6 3	♡ A 9 7 6 3	♡ A 9 7 6 3
◇ 10 6 3	◇ K 10 3	◇ K 10 3	◇ 10 6 3	◇ K 6 3	◇ K 3
♣ A K Q	♣ A K Q	♣ A K Q	♣ A K Q	♣ A K Q	♣ A K Q 9

Hands 1 and 2, where declarer's heart holding fits so well with dummy, always produce nine tricks. If you are going to set declarer, you need to find partner with some useful holding in hearts. That reasoning leads you to Hands 3 through 6, all of which can be set. But how should you tackle them? With Hands 3 and 4, declarer's best play was to start spades while he had a sure entry to dummy, hoping to see the ten of spades fall. A little luck in spades or a good heart split would give him his nine tricks. Against a strong declarer, you can discount these two hands, and focus on 5 and 6.

A club return is fine with Hand 5, but is disastrous with Hand 6. A diamond return loses in both cases. A spade or a heart return looks safe on both hands, and a heart is preferable because it interferes with declarer's communications. If declarer plays a diamond to his king, partner's count signal will tell you how to continue. If he shows three diamonds, you can exit with a club (Hand 5), and if he shows four diamonds (Hand 6) you can return the jack of diamonds. Finally, if declarer returns to hand with a club, partner's card will tell you if declarer started with three or four cards in that suit and you will know whether you are facing Hand 5 or Hand 6.

This deal has many variations. It shows how a defender can build up possible hands for declarer and then avoid committing to an early losing play by waiting until there is enough information to deduce the winning line.

This was the actual deal:

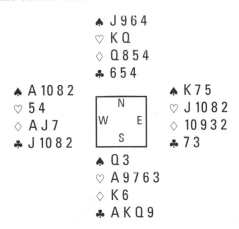

Now let's try another one, this time a deal with some significance in bridge history. This is the bidding (both vulnerable):

WEST	NORTH	EAST	SOUTH
You		*Partner*	
1♣	pass	1◇	3♠
dbl	all pass		

You lead the king of clubs against three spades doubled, and here is what you see as declarer ruffs your club:

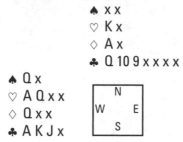

```
              ♠ x x
              ♡ K x
              ◇ A x
              ♣ Q 10 9 x x x x
 ♠ Q x                          N
 ♡ A Q x x                   W     E
 ◇ Q x x                        S
 ♣ A K J x
```

Declarer now leads a low heart from hand and at Trick 2 you have already reached the turning point of the hand. Your double promises plenty of high cards but not a spade stack, so partner needs some defensive values to leave it in. Declarer is vulnerable, so he rates to have a decent seven-card suit. In any case, you can see that with eight trumps he will always take ten tricks. You are therefore going to play declarer for six red-suit cards, distributed either 3-3 or 4-2. If his spades are solid, declarer again has ten tricks, so you must assume partner has the ace or king of spades. Partner should also have the king of diamonds. What does that leave for possible declarer hands?

Hand 1	Hand 2	Hand 3	Hand 4
♠ A J 10 9 x x x	♠ A J 10 9 x x x	♠ K J 10 9 x x x	♠ K J 10 9 x x x
♡ 8 6 5	♡ J 8 6 5	♡ 8 6 5	♡ J 8 6 5
◇ x x x	◇ x x	◇ x x x	◇ x x
♣ —	♣ —	♣ —	♣ —

The defense needed a trump lead to set Hands 1 and 2, and both are cold now, so you might as well focus your energy on Hands 3 and 4. Declarer has eight tricks in both cases, and if he can trump a red-suit card in dummy, he has nine. The defense must lead ace and another trump on gaining the lead. Why not win the ace of hearts right now and lead a spade, then? That works fine against Hand 3, but against Hand 4, on that defense, declarer has good enough heart spots to force a ninth trick. You must duck the heart, and if partner can win the second heart, you must trust that he realizes the necessity of playing ace and another spade.

The whole deal was:

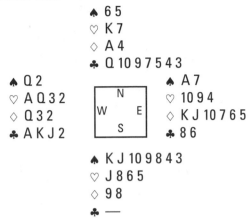

```
                    ♠ 6 5
                    ♡ K 7
                    ◇ A 4
                    ♣ Q 10 9 7 5 4 3
    ♠ Q 2                          ♠ A 7
    ♡ A Q 3 2          N           ♡ 10 9 4
    ◇ Q 3 2       W       E        ◇ K J 10 7 6 5
    ♣ A K J 2         S            ♣ 8 6
                    ♠ K J 10 9 8 4 3
                    ♡ J 8 6 5
                    ◇ 9 8
                    ♣ —
```

This deal determined the outcome of the 1982 World Championship, where the Trick 2 play by West was indeed the turning point. West rose with the ace of hearts to play trumps and the French declarer found the right continuation in hearts (Hand 4). The heart position around the table after West rose with the ace and declarer subsequently played the king was:

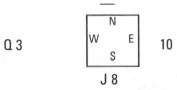

```
              —
              N
Q 3      W       E      10
              S
              J 8
```

When the declarer guessed to lead the jack from hand, smothering the ten, he made his contract, and the American team lost 14 IMPs on the board. Trick 2 on this deal was truly the turning point of the whole World Championship final match because this misdefense led to the US team falling behind. This in turn necessitated an anti-percentage play by an American declarer in a later 3NT contract to try to create a swing. (The anti-percentage play was correct at that stage of the match but resulted in the loss of ten more IMPs). France won the final by 17 IMPs. Of course, a 3NT bid by East on our example deal would have won the championship outright for the Americans.

Our third problem also offers a reward for a thoughtful defender.

```
                      ♠ 4 2
                      ♡ J 10 7
                      ◇ Q 6 4
                      ♣ K Q J 4 2
    ♠ A Q 5 3       ┌─────────────┐
    ♡ 5 3 2         │      N      │
    ◇ 10 7 5 3      │ W         E │
    ♣ A 3           │      S      │
                    └─────────────┘
```

WEST	NORTH	EAST	SOUTH
			1♡
pass	2♡	pass	3♡
pass	4♡	all pass	

You lead your three of diamonds, declarer plays dummy's queen, and partner the king. Declarer wins the diamond ace, cashes the ace of hearts, felling partner's queen, then plays the seven of clubs. What are some possible hands for declarer? He has six hearts, based on partner's queen play. He may or may not have the spade king.

Hand 1	Hand 2	Hand 3
♠ K 9	♠ K 9	♠ 9 7
♡ A K 9 8 6 4	♡ A K 9 8 6 4	♡ A K 9 8 6 4
◇ A 8 2	◇ A 9 8 2	◇ A J 8 2
♣ 7 6	♣ 7	♣ 7

At IMPs, you need four tricks. In addition to your aces, partner needs a diamond trick which will serve as an entry to lead a spade through.

Against Hand 1, you can relax — declarer has only eight tricks. Just remember to lead a diamond when you win the ace of clubs.

Hand 2 requires that you sit up. If you duck a club, declarer can ruff out your ace, cross to dummy while drawing trumps, pitch his spades, and give up two diamonds to make his contract. You must rise with the ace of clubs now and return a diamond. Partner will win the jack and shift to a spade. You can cash two spades and another diamond for down two.

Hand 3 always makes. If you cash spades, declarer uses the clubs to pitch losing diamonds. If you lead a diamond back, declarer will win, draw trumps, and pitch two losing spades and a diamond. You get the last diamond.

Therefore, the defense that covers those hands that can be set is to rise with the ace of clubs, return a diamond, and hope!

The whole deal was:

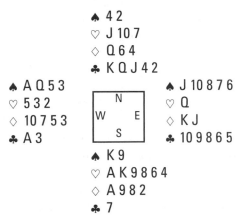

♠ 4 2
♥ J 10 7
♦ Q 6 4
♣ K Q J 4 2

♠ A Q 5 3　　　　　♠ J 10 8 7 6
♥ 5 3 2　　　　　　♥ Q
♦ 10 7 5 3　　　　　♦ K J
♣ A 3　　　　　　　♣ 10 9 8 6 5

♠ K 9
♥ A K 9 8 6 4
♦ A 9 8 2
♣ 7

At matchpoints, you would have to consider cashing out your spade trick(s) and holding declarer to either four or five (depending on who has the king of spades). This line of defense gains a trick against Hand 3 but costs the contract against Hand 2, and an extra downtrick against Hand 1.

PLAYING IN TEMPO

*The expert makes a practice of planning his defense at a time
when no particular inference can be drawn from his pause.*
Marshall Miles, **All Fifty-two Cards.**

One concern of anyone deciding to work on visualization skills will be, 'Am I going to slow down play on every contract I defend?' My answer is, certainly you are. But what if you do? Bridge is a game for thinkers, and no one will achieve consistently good results without investing in thinking time at the table. If you are a slow player, frequently in time trouble, look elsewhere for ways to improve your speed – cut down on discussions at the table or make your comfort breaks more efficient. Don't cut into your thinking time. You have to develop good thinking habits. In defense, that means visualizing the unseen hands, and especially, letting your mind roam over a few alternatives before making a play in a pivotal situation. Unless one is blessed with the lightning speed of an Oswald Jacoby or a Jeff Meckstroth, one needs practice to improve the ability to visualize; that is, players must train themselves to visualize unseen hands in developing defensive plans. With practice and some hard work away from the table, a player can improve his speed of play. Bridge is not a speed contest. No one can play good defense by rushing. The rewarding aspect of all this is that, the harder you work at it, the faster you become at analysis, and (the real payoff) the more accurate you become.

Much defensive card play is second nature to a regular player. It seems routine. But if you kibitz an expert table in a National event, especially the late stages of the Vanderbilt or the Spingold, you will see that the players take plenty of time to work through alternatives. If you have ambitions to become a strong defender, you will invest the time to visualize alternatives in working out the optimum defense on every hand you play. No-one can be perfect, but raising one's average percentage by even a few points means the difference between a journeyman campaigner and a dangerous contender.

SUMMARY OF THE VISUALIZATION PROCESS

The goal of the *visualization* process is to make sure that, as a defender, you consider alternatives broadly enough to make good decisions.

As a defender,

> Start the process at Trick 1. Remember that a hesitation at the key moment may itself cost the contract.

> Form a mental picture of several possible hands for declarer instead of just one hand. Make your picture small enough to get your mind around it, but broad enough that you do not overlook any reasonable possibility for declarer (usually three or four hands).

> Mull over information from the bidding, from partner's lead and signals, and from declarer's tactics. Remember that even at an early stage of a hand there is useful information to help you define your mental picture. Notrump bids, five-card majors, and any number of special conventions are revealing. Leads, signals, and the early play all add vital data.

> With three or four hands in mind, eliminate those that do not belong. If a hand does not jibe with partner's lead and signals, move on. If your count of points and distribution tells you the hand is impossible, throw it out.

> Make the winning play!

CHAPTER 3

Gathering information

"An average player is often startled — even offended — when it is pointed out that, as a defender, he possessed all the necessary tools to count out a hand and conduct a devastating defense." Jake Winkman in 'A Simple Defense'.

Don Von Elsner, **The Best of Jake Winkman**

A defender must have his antenna tuned to receive information from all available broadcasts. The bidding will provide anything from a general to an exact description of the declaring side's distribution and high card strength. You add in information from partner's opening lead, and then, as play progresses, you include data from partner's signals and from the tactics that declarer is adopting. Information gathering is a race against time. The opening lead may determine the outcome of the hand or a good declarer may force a defensive guess early in the hand when information is scarce. Defenders must cope with these situations as best they can. In the vast majority of hands, though, defenders have the time to pick up information from many sources, to process it, and to come to a logical answer as to what their plan should be. In this chapter we will deal with two main sources of information: partnership agreements and counting.

Before reaching for the stars, every partnership has to look after the basic necessities of defense. What are these? Leads and signals, of course. There are plenty of good defensive carding methods to choose from, each with its adherents. My own view is that swings derived solely from the use of one carding method over another occur pretty much at random, with equal numbers going to all sides. On the other hand, lack of solid agreements certainly can result in swings. It is absolutely necessary to be on the same wavelength as partner. The exact nature of your agreements is far less important than discussing and confirming them with partner. Let us take a moment, however, and look at some of the issues worth thinking about when you make those agreements.

OPENING LEAD AGREEMENTS

What do we want from a system of leads? They should:

Generally give partner as much information as possible to guide the defense.

Remove ambiguity for the defenders between leads from AK and KQ.

Provide helpful count information. For example, at suit play it helps to be able to identify doubleton KQ, QJ, and J10 leads, and at notrump, one would like to know if partner has led a short suit (two or three) or from length (four or more).

Indicate the leader's attitude to the suit led.

There are different ways of coping with these problems, and defenders must make choices. One point is clear: old-fashioned standard leads must go. Leading ace from ace-king is sometimes an improvement, and avoids disasters such as the following deal (from a World Championship).

```
                      ♠ A 7 5 4
                      ♡ 10 9 6 4 3
                      ◇ —
                      ♣ K 9 6 2
      ♠ K Q 9                        ♠ J 10 8 6 3 2
      ♡ K Q 8 2         N            ♡ J 7
      ◇ J 2         W       E        ◇ A 8 7
      ♣ A 8 7 5         S            ♣ Q 3
                      ♠ —
                      ♡ A 5
                      ◇ K Q 10 9 6 5 4 3
                      ♣ J 10 4
```

WEST	NORTH	EAST	SOUTH
			1◇
dbl	1♡	2♠	3◇
3♠	pass	4♠	pass
pass	dbl	all pass	

On South's lead of the king of diamonds, North is in a quandary if they lead the king from both king-queen and ace-king combinations. He can set the hand by ruffing and returning a heart for a second ruff, but how does he know this? South could easily hold the ◇AK and no ♡A. In practice, North ducked and the contract made.

Leading ace from AKx(x) solves this kind of problem, but creates others. An ace lead is sometimes a stab — a fond hope that this blind lead will turn out better than other blind leads. Defenders leading the ace from AKx will expect partner to encourage with a queen holding, or against suit contracts, with a doubleton. However, this may be entirely the wrong defense.

Partnerships have a number of choices to make for their opening lead system. Common methods include:

A. Old-fashioned standard (fourth best, top of a sequence of honors, but K from AK)

B. Standard except A from AKx

C. Coded nines and tens (jack denies, ten and nine may show two higher honors)

D. Rusinow: second-highest of touching honors versus suits, and **A** or **C** versus notrump

E. Journalist leads (Rusinow honor leads against suits, standard honor leads against notrump except jack denies a higher honor and ten promises one or two higher honors, attitude spot-card leads against notrump, third-best from even and low from odd against suits)

F. Bridge World Standard leads (**B** honor leads; spot cards are third-best from even and low from odd against suits, fourth best against notrump)

G. The method recommended here: Rusinow honor leads in all situations

When I first started playing Rusinow honor-card leads, I found my partners wanted to retain standard leads against notrump, slams, and when leading partner's suit, so I went along with them. I now much prefer to play Rusinow leads in all situations, and that is the method I recommend. Why are Rusinow leads unpopular against notrump? The argument runs as follows, from *The Official Encyclopedia Of Bridge*, Fifth Edition: 'Against a suit, third hand has to know what specific honors the leader has, so the AK ambiguity has to be resolved. Against notrump, third hand has to know whether partner has led his best suit, that is, whether he has honors in the suit led, not which specific ones they are.' This statement helps a little (very little). I would add, 'The defense benefits by knowing whether opening leader has length in the suit led, as well which honors he has.' A modification to Rusinow leads against notrump only may overcome the difficulty. The modification is to lead highest in a sequence from a short holding (two- or three-card suit), and second highest from a sequence in a longer suit (four or more). This method is discussed more fully later.

In my view, this system has a number of advantages over Journalist leads:

- My lead system blends well with MUD (Middle-Up-Down) leads from three small cards (scorned by many experts yet effective in a vast percentage of real-life hands).

- Leading low (fourth best) from a holding including the ten works against the following common layout:

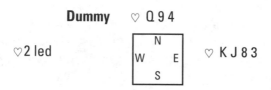

Dummy   ♡ Q 9 4

♡2 led   ♡ K J 8 3

On the lead of the deuce against a suit contract, East knows to play the eight, whereas after a Journalist lead of (say) the deuce (from three small) or the six or seven (from four to the ten or a doubleton), East may make a wrong guess. Against notrump, West may want to play the jack if he thinks partner might have led from Axxx.

Leading second highest from all sequences, including interior sequences, leaves some ambiguity for the declarer. Thus when a defender has bid spades and leads the ten against an eventual three notrump contract, declarer has to guess in this and similar situations:

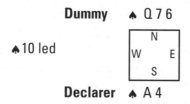

Dummy   ♠ Q 7 6

♠10 led

Declarer   ♠ A 4

Declarer cannot tell whether the lead is from J109x or K109x.

While this system of opening leads solves many problems, it admittedly also creates others.

It gives declarer plenty of information — more than other lead systems. Defensive play is tough enough, however, and I believe defenders need all the help they can get.

In some situations the defenders have a crucial guess. The worst case is the lead of a ten versus a suit contract when the queen appears in dummy. If the nine is visible, you know the lead is from J10x or from shortness. If the nine is hidden, you cannot tell if partner has the king, and you risk the embarrassment of allowing declarer to make his doubleton or (worst of all) singleton jack. Of course, with standard leads, there is ambiguity when partner leads a jack. He could have the king-jack-ten, or declarer could have a singleton king.

The complete system that I recommend is outlined below.

Leads against suit contracts

- Honor leads show one higher honor or shortness (doubleton or singleton) in the suit.

- Spot card leads from strength (honor holding of ten or better) are fourth best.

- High from a doubleton.

- Second highest from a worthless holding (three, four or five small).

- From three small in partner's suit: high if you supported, low if you did not.

What about third and fifth leads against suits, a method that has gained some popularity in recent years? Every now and then a partnership benefits from the knowledge at Trick 1 that partner has exactly three or exactly five cards in a suit. Indeed, the leads from an odd number are fine, but from a four-card suit they often become impossible for partner to fathom. Say partner has a holding of K872; he must lead the seven, and the defense may lose a valuable tempo working out the true attitude of the opening leader. Third and fifth leads are also incompatible with the style of 'second highest from worthless holdings.' If you play third and fifth leads, you pretty much have to settle for lowest from a bad holding, misleading partner about attitude, or highest from a bad three- or four-card holding, misleading partner about length. The problem here too is that your high spot card may blow a trick outright; for instance, in this well-known situation, the lead of the nine costs a trick:

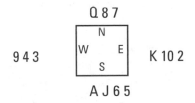

Q 8 7

9 4 3   K 10 2

A J 6 5

Occasionally, too, the lead of an eight or nine wastes a card that could prevent a squeeze (see pages 110-113). However, my major objection to leading highest from worthless holdings is that partner never knows when you have a doubleton, and that may be key information in suit contracts.

Leads against notrump contracts

- Spot card leads are fourth best, except that leads from worthless holdings are second highest.

- From three small in partner's suit, lead high if you supported or low if you did not.

- Honor leads show one higher honor with length (four or more) or no higher honors (with three or fewer cards in the suit).

This last convention is intended to avoid the embarrassment of setting up declarer's own suit for him. Consider the following deal:

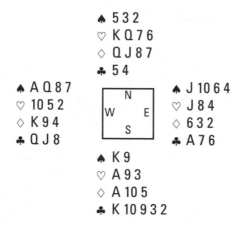

```
                    ♠ 5 3 2
                    ♡ K Q 7 6
                    ◇ Q J 8 7
                    ♣ 5 4
    ♠ A Q 8 7            N            ♠ J 10 6 4
    ♡ 10 5 2       W          E       ♡ J 8 4
    ◇ K 9 4                           ◇ 6 3 2
    ♣ Q J 8             S             ♣ A 7 6
                    ♠ K 9
                    ♡ A 9 3
                    ◇ A 10 5
                    ♣ K 10 9 3 2
```

After declarer has opened one notrump and bought the contract, if partner leads the club jack you will surely overtake (could be KJ10xx) and return a club. Embarrassing! If your understanding is that partner's queen lead suggests the king with four or more, and the jack with three or fewer, you play the seven, and when the king is quickly revealed in declarer's hand, a spade shift will be easy to find later on.

The lead of an ace against notrump

The lead of an ace against notrump contracts is either a stab (say against a Gambling 3NT or against some other contract where leader has no good suit and wants to hit partner) or else shows a big holding in that suit such as AQJ10x *or* AKJ10x *or* AKJxx *or* AKQxx.

I recommend the following agreement: the ace asks for an unblock of the king or queen, asks for the jack from J10x, and otherwise requests count. This last addition is needed to avoid the embarrassment of taking only four tricks when the defenders hold AKQxx opposite J10xx. On a bad day, defenders have been known to take only three tricks with this holding after a double unblock sets up declarer's nine!

SUMMARY OF RECOMMENDED OPENING LEADS

Card led	Against notrump contracts, the lead shows	Against suit contracts, the lead shows
Ace	Asks for unblock of K or Q, play of J from J10+, otherwise count, or a stab	Shortness or a stab
King	AK(xx) or KQx or Kx	AK(x) or shortness
Queen	KQ10(x) or QJx or Qx	KQ(x) or shortness
Jack	AJ10(x) KJ10(x) QJ10x(x) or J10x or Jx	KJ10(x) QJ10(x) or shortness
Ten	A109(x) K109(x) Q109(x) J109x(x) 109x or 10x	K109(x) Q109(x) J109(x) or shortness
Nine	109xx(x) or 9x	109x(x) or shortness
Spot cards from worthless holding	Second highest from holdings of three or more small cards	Second highest from holdings of three or more small cards
Spot cards in partner's suit	If supported, highest from three If unsupported, lowest from three	If supported, highest from three If unsupported, lowest from three
Spot cards from honor holding of 10 or better	Low from three Otherwise fourth best	Low from three Otherwise fourth best

DEFENSIVE SIGNALING

Defensive signals are important in supplementing good thinking but do not replace it. Again, there are many good systems and agreements available, and again, there is not as much to choose between them as some of their adherents would have you believe. I have been involved in fine defenses using various methods of signaling, and always go along with partner's preferences. Given free choice, however, the methods that I prefer and recommend are as follows:

> **Attitude**: standard (high-low encourages)
>
> **Count:** standard (high-low shows an even number)
>
> **Suit preference:** high suggests preference for higher-ranking suit. Frequent suit-preference signals are vital in eliminating guesswork for defenders.
>
> **Trump Echo:** show three or five trumps by playing high-low. You do this especially if you want a ruff, or whenever you think trump count is unclear and a signal may help partner.
>
> **Remainder (present) count:** high-low shows even number remaining.
>
> **Smith Echo:** high-low in the first suit declarer plays (against both suits and notrump) suggests the opening lead was good.

The two fundamental principles of signaling, which apply whether you're playing standard or upside-down signals, are:

- Always signal with the highest card you can afford
- Do not waste a trick when signaling.

A common problem occurs where a defender holds a tenace and a small card over dummy or declarer.

```
                    Q x x
                  ┌───────┐
                  │   N   │
        A x x x   │ W   E │   K J x
                  │   S   │
                  └───────┘
                   10 x x
```

When you lead the ace in this situation, be aware that partner cannot waste the jack as a signal. Your decision to continue or not will have to be based on considerations of the whole deal. No squirming by East, please!

SIGNAL PRIORITY

'I wanted to say that if you had six spades, cash the ace and give me a ruff, but with five spades switch to diamonds, if you had an honor, otherwise lead a low heart but don't lead trumps. It was kinda hard to say all that with a nine.'
Table Talk, Jude Goodwin-Hansen.

An issue that trips up many defenders is determining what a signal means in a given situation. Is that nine encouraging, or is it a count card, or could it somehow be indicating suit preference, or is it something else entirely? This issue is called **signal priority**. These are the thoughts to keep in mind when judging signal priority:

- Attitude has priority, except for contracts at the five-level and higher.

- At the five-level and higher, or when attitude is known, count has priority.

- When attitude is known, and count is irrelevant, suit preference has priority.

- In other cases Smith Echo has priority. (Many players apply Smith only against notrump, but I recommend using it against suit contracts as well. Just keep it in its right place on the priority list.)

Understanding priorities is fundamental to good signaling. Modern signaling has evolved to a (sometimes) confusing methodology where a card means one thing one time, and another the next. The only way to sort out these meanings is to keep one's priorities firmly in mind. Thus, suit preference only applies after attitude and count are out of the question, and Smith Echo lags behind everything.

A few examples will help you through the minefield associated with signaling. Be prepared for disasters as you work out the methods with your favorite partner. First, here is an amusing deal that steered me away from upside-down signals forever, although I still agree to play them with partners who have strong feelings on the subject. I became declarer after partner had opened one spade and then raised my one notrump response to game. After the ten of hearts lead, East won the ace, laid down the club ace, and received the screaming two, which encouraged him to continue the suit.

Unfortunately for him, this was the layout:

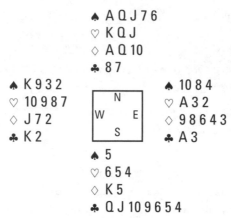

♠ A Q J 7 6
♡ K Q J
◇ A Q 10
♣ 8 7

♠ K 9 3 2   ♠ 10 8 4
♡ 10 9 8 7   ♡ A 3 2
◇ J 7 2   ◇ 9 8 6 4 3
♣ K 2   ♣ A 3

♠ 5
♡ 6 5 4
◇ K 5
♣ Q J 10 9 6 5 4

East needed to shift to diamonds after winning the ace of hearts, and the defender winning the first club needed to continue diamonds. On that defense my cause would have been hopeless.

Here is another example which has influenced (clouded) my thinking.

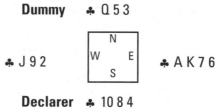

Dummy   ♣ Q 5 3

♣ J 9 2   ♣ A K 7 6

Declarer   ♣ 10 8 4

Desperate for one club trick while playing against opponents using upside-down signals, I led the three of clubs from dummy; right-hand opponent won the king, and left-hand opponent played the nine. Now I could finesse the ten for my vital club trick. Yes, East had a difficult decision on the play of a club, but rising with the king was not fatal. The signal was the killer. Of course, advocates of upside-down signals can recall the equally outlandish results that led to their own conversions.

I find also that when I am playing upside-down signals, partner and I tend to signal much more often than playing standard methods. This gives enormous help to declarers. As well, upside-down signals seem to offer fewer opportunities for deception than regular methods (or perhaps declarers ignore my efforts.) However, there is little to choose between upside-down and standard systems, and the moral is: do what partner is comfortable with. The real keys in signaling are to be on the same wavelength as partner, to have a clear idea of signaling priorities, and to use every opportunity for suit preference signals.

SUIT PREFERENCE SIGNALS

We are all taught the routine suit-preference situation where we are giving partner a ruff and he needs to know how to get back to our hand for another ruff. However, experts use suit preference signals in many situations, especially when following suit at a time where the order of the cards they play doesn't matter. In this example, defenders make use of otherwise meaningless spot cards to indicate the right defense.

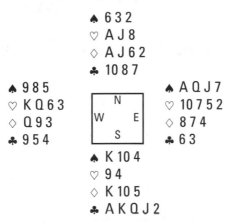

```
                    ♠ 6 3 2
                    ♡ A J 8
                    ◇ A J 6 2
                    ♣ 10 8 7
        ♠ 9 8 5                       ♠ A Q J 7
        ♡ K Q 6 3      N              ♡ 10 7 5 2
        ◇ Q 9 3    W       E          ◇ 8 7 4
        ♣ 9 5 4        S              ♣ 6 3
                    ♠ K 10 4
                    ♡ 9 4
                    ◇ K 10 5
                    ♣ A K Q J 2
```

After a quick 1NT — 3NT, you lead the three of hearts to dummy's eight, partner's ten and declarer's four. Partner continues with the ♡2 to your queen, and declarer holds up. You continue with the ♡6 and declarer wins, pitching the ◇5 from his hand. He plays a diamond to his ten and your queen. You cash the king of hearts, and declarer pitches the four of spades. What next?

You can infer that declarer is not going to run away with the spade suit after his discard. Why is he playing diamonds and leaving clubs untouched? Partner should play the seven, then five of hearts, in following to the ace and then your king of hearts, indicating an interest in the spade suit. Then you'll have no difficulty making the right play.

Plays like this are an extension of normal suit-preference signals, and opportunities to use them occur frequently. They help sort out hands where one partner may be faced with a blind guess as he looks for the setting trick.

On this next deal, you are defending a five-level contract and having to sort out signaling priorities.

♠ Q x
♡ x
◇ A Q J x x x
♣ A K Q x

♠ K x x
♡ J 10 9 x
◇ x x
♣ J x x x

WEST	NORTH	EAST	SOUTH
PARTNER		*YOU*	
			2♠
pass	2NT	pass	3◇[1]
pass	4NT[2]	pass	5♣[3]
pass	5♠	all pass	

1. Feature and good hand
2. Roman key card Blackwood
3. One or four key cards.

Partner leads the ♡K, and your jack should invite a continuation, so that your king of spades is protected. True, count has priority at the five-level and higher, but here count is irrelevant. Change the hand slightly with the same auction:

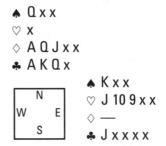

♠ Q x x
♡ x
◇ A Q J x x
♣ A K Q x

♠ K x x
♡ J 10 9 x x
◇ —
♣ J x x x x

Here a heart continuation is pointless. Count is irrelevant in the heart suit, and attitude is known, so priority switches to suit preference. A diamond switch stops the overtrick, and gives you a chance to beat the contract, so you play the jack of hearts at Trick 1. You ruff partner's diamond and play a club to dummy. Now, declarer will occasionally fly with the ace of spades after leading the spade queen from dummy (naturally you do not cover), especially if you play high-low in trumps, showing three and suggesting that you can ruff another diamond.

SIGNALS IN THE TRUMP SUIT

This brings us neatly to the topic of signaling in the trump suit. The main theme associated with trump-suit signals is showing count in trumps. A trump echo (high-low) is normally used to indicate count in trumps in a ruffing situation. In some cases, suit-preference or Smith Echo can be signaled instead. Defenders must have a clear idea of their priorities in signaling with trumps. These are:

- Count in trumps to indicate a ruff or a second ruff has priority

- When count is known, or a ruff is known not to be lurking, suit preference has priority

- When count is known and suit preference is irrelevant, Smith becomes the priority.

In both of the following examples the bidding has gone:

WEST	NORTH	EAST	SOUTH
			1♠
pass	2♠	pass	pass
dbl	redbl	3♡	pass
pass	3♠	all pass	

You (West) lead the queen of hearts. Dummy wins the ace as partner plays the jack. Declarer then runs dummy's jack of spades to your king.

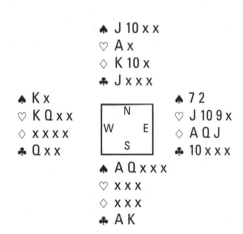

East's card here is important, since you (West) are bound to have some guesswork when you win your spade trick. East's count in trumps is known, and there is no possible ruff in sight, so priority must switch to suit preference. East should play the seven of spades under the jack, telling you to shift to a diamond right away, and to preserve your heart as an entry to lead a second round of diamonds.

Change the East hand slightly:

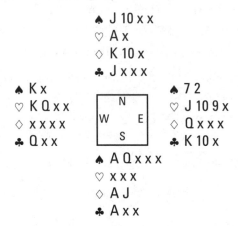

Now a club shift is best and East should play the two of spades under the jack. An immediate diamond shift hands declarer an overtrick. After a club shift, declarer must risk his contract if he tries for an overtrick. A corollary of this reasoning is that good declarers must make use of their spot cards to disguise the nature of these signals as much as possible. In the examples chosen the seven and two of trumps could not be mistaken. In real life you don't always get such unequivocal holdings. Nonetheless, defenders must take advantage when they can.

A final variation on the theme of signaling in the trump suit:

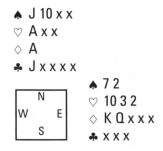

After an uncontested auction where the opponents bid 1♠-3♠-4♠, West (partner) leads the jack of hearts, promising the queen. Declarer wins the ace and you signal with the three, which partner is sure to have difficulty reading. When declarer plays the jack of spades from dummy, you play the seven, intending this as a Smith Echo, indicating that you like hearts. This cannot be mistaken for a trump echo (you cannot have three trumps) or a suit-preference play suggesting diamonds (a pointless shift). You may stop an overtrick if partner continues hearts.

COUNT, COUNT, COUNT

"It is possible to be a reasonably good declarer without bothering to count the hands. However, it is absolutely essential to attempt to count the unseen hands when you are defending." **All Fifty-Two cards,** Marshall Miles.

Counting points and distribution is a fundamental skill needed by every defender. I offer two examples to show how counting meshes with visualization and reconstruction of unseen hands. Some folks say 'I don't count every hand, only those that are important.' I say, 'How do you know in advance which hand is going to be important?' Regular counting of every hand helps to improve your counting skill. You absolutely want accuracy and speed in counting, so do it on every hand — even when you are dummy. There is a particular angle to counting that is important to defenders. As you count declarer's points and distribution and reconstruct his holding, make the assumption that he can be set on every hand (at least when you are playing IMPs). If you place him with an eight-card suit, and you see that his contract is then cold, assume only a seven-card suit. If the hand is still cold, imagine a six-bagger. If you can visualize setting a hand only with a five-card main suit, then defend on that basis.

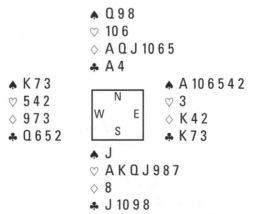

```
              ♠ Q 9 8
              ♡ 10 6
              ♢ A Q J 10 6 5
              ♣ A 4
♠ K 7 3                      ♠ A 10 6 5 4 2
♡ 5 4 2          N           ♡ 3
♢ 9 7 3      W     E         ♢ K 4 2
♣ Q 6 5 2        S           ♣ K 7 3
              ♠ J
              ♡ A K Q J 9 8 7
              ♢ 8
              ♣ J 10 9 8
```

After you overcall North's 1♢ with 1♠, South jumps in hearts and you end up defending against six hearts. Partner (West) leads the ♠3 to your ace and declarer's jack. You can see that if declarer has a doubleton diamond, the defense has no worries. Give her a singleton diamond, and now what hands give you any chance? With eight solid hearts, the contract is cold (via a ruffing finesse in diamonds, with the ten of hearts and ace of clubs for entries.) With seven hearts and a singleton diamond, the contract makes unless you get rid of an entry to dummy right now by leading a club. If declarer has the club queen, too bad; your shift will give her two club tricks, and she can ruff two clubs in dummy. However, in that case, she was about to make the hand in any case when partner did not lead a club. You must base your defense on a hand that needs some defensive work (singleton diamond in South), and a holding that can go down (seven trumps only, no queen of clubs in declarer's hand). On the deal shown, a shift to the king of clubs also works, but a low club is better because declarer will sometimes hold the ♣Q10 and misguess.

Now here's an example of counting and reconstruction at its best.

```
              ♠ A J 7 2
              ♡ 2
              ◇ A K Q 8 3
              ♣ K J 5
                              ♠ K 4
            ┌─────────┐       ♡ J 10
            │    N    │       ◇ 10 9 7 5 2
            │ W     E │       ♣ A 9 8 3
            │    S    │
            └─────────┘
```

WEST	NORTH	EAST	SOUTH
PARTNER		*YOU*	
2♡	dbl	pass	2♠
pass	3♠	pass	4♠
all pass			

Partner leads the king of hearts and declarer wins the ace. Declarer then plays a low spade to the jack. You win and think about the defense.

Hand 1	Hand 2	Hand 3	Hand 4	Hand 5
♠ 10 9 8 6 5	♠ Q 10 8 5	♠ Q 8 5 3	♠ Q 8 5 3	♠ Q 9 8 5
♡ A 8 6 5	♡ A 8 6 5	♡ A 8 6 5	♡ A 8 6 5	♡ A 8 6 5
◇ 6	◇ 4	◇ J	◇ 6	◇ 6
♣ 7 6 4	♣ 7 6 4 2	♣ 7 6 4 2	♣ 10 6 4 2	♣ 7 6 4 2

You infer that if partner had a minor-suit singleton he would have led it, and so his distribution is most likely 6-3-2-2. You can work out that if declarer has any five spades (Hand 1), he will make eleven tricks (four trumps, the ace of hearts and two ruffs, the ace, king, queen of diamonds and a club — he will likely guess the club position). You make your first assumption — that declarer has only four spades. Therefore, partner's distribution is more than likely three spades, six hearts, and a doubleton in each minor. If declarer's spades are headed by the queen-ten (Hand 2), he can always make his contract by reversing the dummy: ruffing one diamond low and one high, and arranging his transportation so that he avoids an overruff position and is in dummy to draw the last trump. So you make your second assumption — that partner has the ten of spades. You can now count nine tricks for declarer: three spades, the ace of hearts and a heart ruff, three diamonds and a club. You see that partner must also have the jack of diamonds; otherwise that is declarer's tenth trick (Hand 3). If declarer's clubs are headed by as little as the ten (Hand 4), he can always manage two club tricks, enough to make his contract. If he has both the queen and the ten, he can take eleven tricks. Therefore, partner must have both the queen and ten of clubs.

This reasoning leads you to Hand 5. Here, a spade return now would pick up partner's ten and allow the dummy reversal. A heart return at Trick 3 would force declarer to ruff in dummy and follow with two rounds of trumps. Unfortunately, you have no idle card to play on the third trump. A diamond discard allows the diamonds to be set up with one ruff and a club pitch lets declarer make two club tricks.

The best return at this point against Hand 5, then, is a low diamond, cutting declarer's communications. Declarer's only hope now is to find diamonds splitting four-three, and he will draw trumps ending in dummy. No doubt he will be disappointed to see your partner follow to the third trump because that means that the chances of diamonds breaking are virtually zero. He will ruff a diamond anyway, hoping for a miracle, but must concede one down gracefully*.

This is the kind of counting (adding and subtracting points and cards in declarer's hand) that pays big dividends for defenders. It goes hand in hand with visualization.

The whole deal appears on the next page.

*See note after diagram on the next page.

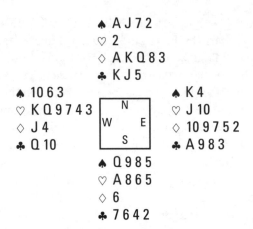

```
              ♠ A J 7 2
              ♡ 2
              ◇ A K Q 8 3
              ♣ K J 5
♠ 10 6 3                          ♠ K 4
♡ K Q 9 7 4 3    ┌─ N ─┐         ♡ J 10
◇ J 4           W        E        ◇ 10 9 7 5 2
♣ Q 10          └─ S ─┘          ♣ A 9 8 3
              ♠ Q 9 8 5
              ♡ A 8 6 5
              ◇ 6
              ♣ 7 6 4 2
```

Note to double dummy analysts: declarer could still make the hand after your diamond play at Trick 3 by cashing exactly one more diamond before drawing the last trump. Then he leads a club to dummy, covers partner's card, and lets partner hold the club which you return. Partner has only hearts left, and you are impaled on a suicide trump squeeze. Hats off to the declarer who finds this line.

CHAPTER 4

WHAT ARE DEFENDER'S TACTICS?

The outstanding characteristic of defensive play in duplicate bridge is that you can never relax. There is almost no such thing as an unimportant contract.

Ely Culbertson, **Bidding and Play at Duplicate Contract Bridge**

Think of the types of play you engage in when you are declarer: trump some losers; reverse the dummy; crossruff; set up a side suit; make an endplay or a squeeze. These plays are all well documented in bridge literature and are understood by a wide circle of players.

Defenders, too, have a range of plays available; most players, whatever their level of competence, are aware of some typical defensive tactical moves. Few players, however, recognize which one to apply at the right time, and even fewer are skilled in visualizing alternative declarer hands as part of a routine process to work out a good defense. If you say to your friends, 'How do you get a ruff for partner on this hand?', you will get mostly right answers, regardless of how unusual your problem. And if you now ask, 'How do you stop a dummy reversal on this one?' you will get plenty of good responses. But if you ask a more open-ended question such as, 'How do you defend this hand?', the membership of the charmed circle who answer correctly shrinks drastically. Players who are excellent declarers often flounder on defense because they have not trained themselves to visualize alternatives.

Every ambitious defender must learn the tactics of defense and keep them at his fingertips. The time you invest in this effort will make defense in real life much easier. Here is a simple list of tactics which should cover a high percentage of the hands you encounter.

Defending against suits

- preventing declarer's ruffs
- getting defensive ruffs
- promoting defensive trump tricks
- making the defensive trumps separately
- forcing declarer (sometimes dummy) to ruff
- killing dummy's long suit
- preventing an endplay
- breaking up a squeeze
- cashing out

- setting up the defenders' best suit
- switching usefully
- cutting declarer's communications
- preventing an endplay
- breaking up a squeeze
- cashing out

Nine tactical choices in suit contracts, and six against notrump. Three items occur in both notrump and suit play, but they have different quirks so we shall look at them separately. I encourage readers to master this lot and then make their own list.

I will run through an example of each of the tactics listed above. My purpose here is to help cement the concept in the reader's mind, so you will not find a comprehensive discussion of the many variations that are possible with each ploy. As you go through the hands and analysis in this section, notice how much easier than real life the problems are, because the right tactic is identified for you before the play starts. At the table, you have to work out the hand type you are dealing with and then apply the right tactic.

DEFENDING AGAINST SUITS

PREVENTING A RUFF

There are many hands where a trump lead is undesirable (singleton trump, trump honor, fear of picking up partner's trick, fear of losing a tempo). Hands with a ruff prevention theme often are hopeless without a trump lead at Trick 1, but sometimes the defense has time to recover anyway.

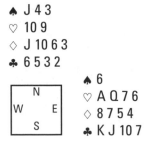

♠ J 4 3
♡ 10 9
◇ J 10 6 3
♣ 6 5 3 2

♠ 6
♡ A Q 7 6
◇ 8 7 5 4
♣ K J 10 7

WEST	NORTH	EAST	SOUTH
Partner		_You_	
			1♠
2◇	pass	3♠[1]	4♠
pass	pass	dbl	all pass

1.   Splinter, sound limit raise.

Partner leads the king of diamonds, and declarer ruffs. He then leads a low heart which you win with the queen. Justify your aggressive double!

Hand 1	Hand 2	Hand 3	Hand 4
♠ A K Q 9 8 7 5	♠ A Q 10 9 8 7 5	♠ A K Q 9 8 7 5	♠ A K Q 9 8 7 5
♡ J 3 2	♡ 8 5 3 2	♡ 8 5 3	♡ J 8 3 2
◇ —	◇ —	◇ —	◇ —
♣ A 9 4	♣ A Q	♣ A Q 9	♣ A 9

Declarer has good spades, no doubt seven of them headed by two or three top honors. He has either three or four hearts – probably four, because partner did not make a takeout double. He has some strength in clubs, it is not clear exactly what. However, it is clear that clubs can not go anywhere.

With this bit of information, you must make a decision at Trick 3. If he has Hand 1, declarer has nine tricks; you can snooze through the defense. With Hand 2, declarer has six spades, two clubs, and one or two heart ruffs; if you don't lead a trump right now, you made a bad double. If he has Hand 3, you did make a bad double. Hand 4 needs an immediate trump return; partner must win the king of hearts, and lead a second trump. The critical hands are 2 and 4, and they both require a trump from you now. Partner will win the second heart and lead a second trump.

Notice the stakes involved. At matchpoints, you are gambling a top versus a bottom, about four percentage points in your ranking. At IMPs, you are looking at losing 13 IMPs, versus gaining perhaps 5. An 18-IMP decision!

The real-life full deal was:

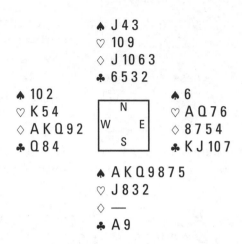

♠ J 4 3
♡ 10 9
◇ J 10 6 3
♣ 6 5 3 2

♠ 10 2
♡ K 5 4
◇ A K Q 9 2
♣ Q 8 4

♠ 6
♡ A Q 7 6
◇ 8 7 5 4
♣ K J 10 7

♠ A K Q 9 8 7 5
♡ J 8 3 2
◇ —
♣ A 9

GETTING A RUFF

The process of a short-suit lead (singleton or occasionally doubleton), a suit-preference signal on the return, then a ruff or second ruff is well documented. An interesting off-shoot lies in finding an unexpected ruff.

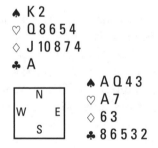

♠ K 2
♡ Q 8 6 5 4
◇ J 10 8 7 4
♣ A

♠ A Q 4 3
♡ A 7
◇ 6 3
♣ 8 6 5 3 2

WEST	NORTH	EAST	SOUTH
Partner		*You*	
			1NT
pass	2◇[1]	pass	2♡
pass	3◇	pass	3♡
pass	4♡	all pass	

1. Transfer to hearts.

Partner leads the ◇9. You don't often expect to give partner a ruff when he leads your short suit! Nevertheless, keep the possibility open. Declarer wins the queen, plays to dummy's ace of clubs (partner plays the queen), then leads a heart. What next? You know that declarer has the king of clubs and a spade is about to disappear from dummy. Partner could afford a club honor, so his holding is solid and only one spade will be discarded. Partner chose to lead dummy's suit instead of a club from a suit headed by the QJ10, normally an attractive holding to lead. What does all this mean?

Hand 1	**Hand 2**
♠ J 7 6	♠ 9 8 7
♡ K J 9	♡ K J 10
◇ A K Q 5 2	◇ A K Q 5
♣ K 7	♣ K 7 4

You know quite a bit about the hand by Trick 3. For his fifteen to seventeen points, declarer needs all the outstanding high cards in the red suits: king, jack of hearts and ace, king, queen of diamonds. Back to partner's play: the only reason he would lead a diamond with a solid club holding is that he had a singleton. Surely the layout is as in Hand 1; therefore, you rise with the ace of hearts and lead a diamond.

The whole deal is as follows:

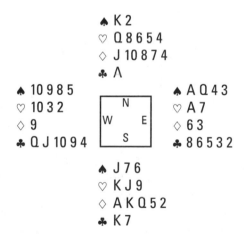

```
                    ♠ K 2
                    ♡ Q 8 6 5 4
                    ◇ J 10 8 7 4
                    ♣ A
    ♠ 10 9 8 5              ♠ A Q 4 3
    ♡ 10 3 2        N       ♡ A 7
    ◇ 9          W     E    ◇ 6 3
    ♣ Q J 10 9 4     S      ♣ 8 6 5 3 2
                    ♠ J 7 6
                    ♡ K J 9
                    ◇ A K Q 5 2
                    ♣ K 7
```

Your play results in a one-trick set.

TRUMP PROMOTION

In some tournaments, trump promotion plays seem to come by the bushel. If you find them all you will earn plenty of matchpoints (or IMPs). Try this one.

♠ A Q J 10
♡ 8 7 4 2
◇ A K 5
♣ 5 4

♠ K 8 5 4 3
♡ A K
◇ 6 4
♣ 10 7 3 2

WEST	NORTH	EAST	SOUTH
Partner		*You*	
	1◇	pass	1♡
pass	2♡	pass	4♡
all pass			

Partner leads the ♠9, and declarer ducks this to your king. Since you know this is a trump promotion hand, you have no problem with the defense, right? However, ignoring that, let us follow our disciplined approach and construct a few possible hands for declarer.

Hand 1	Hand 2	Hand 3	Hand 4
♠ 7 6	♠ 7 6	♠ 7 6	♠ 7 6
♡ Q J 9 6 5 3	♡ Q J 6 5	♡ Q 10 9 3	♡ Q J 10 9 3
◇ 7 3 2	◇ 7 3 2	◇ 7 3	◇ Q 7
♣ A K	♣ A K Q 8	♣ A K Q 8 6	♣ A Q J 8

Hand 1 is cold for ten tricks, but here partner has a singleton in trumps and holds QJ10xx of diamonds. He certainly would not have led a spade. Hands 2 and 3, where partner has 10xx or Jxx in trumps, can be set via a trump promotion, so win the king of spades and return a spade. Lead another when you win the king of trumps and try again, if necessary, when you win the ace of trumps.

You can set Hand 4 with a club shift, but declarer would not have ducked the first spade with this hand. He would have won the spade ace and played three rounds of diamonds to get rid of his spade loser before tackling trumps.

The actual deal was:

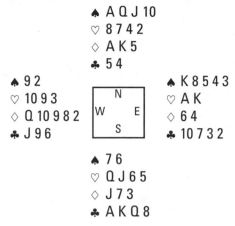

```
              ♠ A Q J 10
              ♡ 8 7 4 2
              ◇ A K 5
              ♣ 5 4
♠ 9 2                        ♠ K 8 5 4 3
♡ 10 9 3         N          ♡ A K
◇ Q 10 9 8 2   W   E        ◇ 6 4
♣ J 9 6          S          ♣ 10 7 3 2
              ♠ 7 6
              ♡ Q J 6 5
              ◇ J 7 3
              ♣ A K Q 8
```

MAKING DEFENSIVE HIGH TRUMPS SEPARATELY

T his tactic is in the same family as trump promotion, but has an interesting character all its own.

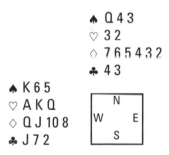

```
              ♠ Q 4 3
              ♡ 3 2
              ◇ 7 6 5 4 3 2
              ♣ 4 3
♠ K 6 5
♡ A K Q          N
◇ Q J 10 8     W   E
♣ J 7 2          S
```

WEST	NORTH	EAST	SOUTH
You		*Partner*	
			1♡
1NT	pass	pass	2♡
pass	pass	dbl[1]	all pass

1.   Maximum values for the previous pass.

You lead the diamond jack, partner plays the ace, then the king. Declarer ruffs this, and leads a heart to your queen. What next?

Hand 1

♠ A J
♡ J 10 9 8 7 6 5
◇ 9
♣ A K Q

Hand 2

♠ A J 5
♡ 10 9 8 7 6 5
◇ 9
♣ A K Q

Declarer needs six or seven hearts and a good club holding without length (or he might have rebid two clubs) to justify his bidding. He should have a spade loser. Partner has shown the ace, king of diamonds, and cannot have much more than that after he passed your 1NT bid. If declarer has Hand 1, you owe partner one for leaving in the double. You must play for Hand 2, giving partner the jack of hearts, and you must play another diamond so that partner can score the heart jack for your sixth trick.

The whole deal was:

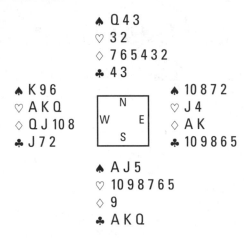

```
              ♠ Q 4 3
              ♡ 3 2
              ◇ 7 6 5 4 3 2
              ♣ 4 3
  ♠ K 9 6                    ♠ 10 8 7 2
  ♡ A K Q          N         ♡ J 4
  ◇ Q J 10 8   W       E     ◇ A K
  ♣ J 7 2          S         ♣ 10 9 8 6 5
              ♠ A J 5
              ♡ 10 9 8 7 6 5
              ◇ 9
              ♣ A K Q
```

FORCING DECLARER

There are hands where a forcing defense causes declarer to lose control of a hand even when he has combined assets of 30 high card points or more. There are situations where a 4-4 fit can be attacked successfully, gaining control by forcing first one hand, then the other, if the timing is handled properly. In the following deal a modest 4-3-2 in the trump suit causes declarer to lose control, because the defenders have a good attacking suit and declarer has too much work to do.

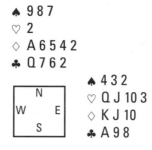

♠ 9 8 7
♡ 2
◇ A 6 5 4 2
♣ Q 7 6 2

♠ 4 3 2
♡ Q J 10 3
◇ K J 10
♣ A 9 8

WEST	NORTH	EAST	SOUTH
Partner		*You*	
			1♡
pass	1NT	pass	2♠
pass	2NT	pass	3♠
pass	4♠	all pass	

Partner leads the jack of clubs, showing a higher honor. What is your plan?

Hand 1	Hand 2	Hand 3	Hand 4
♠ A K 10 6 5	♠ A K J 6 5	♠ A Q J 10 6	♠ A K Q J 6
♡ A K 9 8 7 5	♡ A 9 8 7 5 4	♡ A K 9 8 7 5	♡ A 9 8 7 5 4
◇ 3	◇ 3	◇ 3	◇ 3
♣ 3	♣ 3	♣ 3	♣ 3

You play the nine to encourage partner to continue and declarer ruffs the second round of clubs. With Hand 1, he can ruff a heart, come to his hand with a high spade, cash another spade discovering the good news, draw the last trump, and concede a heart to make eleven tricks. If he has Hand 2, he plays the ace of hearts, and then ruffs out partner's king. Next, he crosses to ace of spades and plays another heart, ruffing in dummy. (Partner must not ruff this with his queen, because that will leave dummy with a trump which declarer can use for transportation.) Declarer now must force himself with either a club or a diamond. You hold declarer to nine tricks: five trumps in hand, the ace of hearts, two ruffs, and the ace of diamonds.

Hand 3 is similar. Declarer's best line is the spade finesse at Trick 5. Partner will win the finesse and should continue a third club. If declarer ducks this to retain control, you have a choice of leading a diamond and making declarer force himself, or leading a trump so that declarer cannot ruff another heart. If declarer has solid spades, as in Hand 4, partner needs the king of hearts to set the contract. If declarer has that card, he makes five.

The actual deal was:

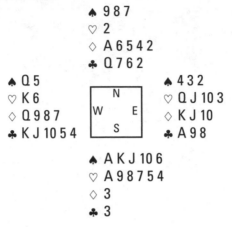

```
              ♠ 9 8 7
              ♡ 2
              ◇ A 6 5 4 2
              ♣ Q 7 6 2
♠ Q 5                        ♠ 4 3 2
♡ K 6          N            ♡ Q J 10 3
◇ Q 9 8 7    W   E          ◇ K J 10
♣ K J 10 5 4     S          ♣ A 9 8
              ♠ A K J 10 6
              ♡ A 9 8 7 5 4
              ◇ 3
              ♣ 3
```

FORCING DUMMY

Defenders sometimes find an opportunity to 'tap' the dummy — they force declarer to ruff early in dummy and thereby use an entry before he really wants to.

```
              ♠ 5 3
              ♡ Q 7 5 3
              ◇ K Q J 10 5 3
              ♣ J
```
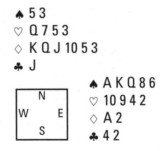
```
                            ♠ A K Q 8 6
                N          ♡ 10 9 4 2
              W   E        ◇ A 2
                S          ♣ 4 2
```

WEST	NORTH	EAST	SOUTH
PARTNER		*You*	
			1♣
pass	1◇	1♠	2♡
pass	4♡	all pass	

Partner leads the two of spades, then plays the ten as you cash a second top spade. What can declarer have? Your partner guarantees an odd number of spades, so he has three here, and so does declarer. Consider these possibilities:

Hand 1	Hand 2	Hand 3	Hand 4
♠ J 9 7	♠ J 9 7	♠ J 9 7	♠ J 9 7
♡ A K J 6	♡ A K J 6	♡ A K J 6	♡ A K 8 6
◇ 9	◇ 9	◇ —	◇ 9
♣ A K Q 9 7	♣ A K 9 7 5	♣ A K 9 7 5 3	♣ A K Q 9 7

Against Hand 1, the defense cannot stop declarer from taking ten tricks: four trumps, a diamond, a spade ruff in dummy, and four clubs.

Against Hand 2, where declarer is light for his reverse, the defense can give declarer serious problems. One tap of dummy's trumps interferes with declarer's communication. When you win the first diamond and play another spade, declarer's percentage line is to ruff high and play for 3-2 trumps, but this line fails.

Against Hand 3, a spade continuation at Trick 3 is still best. Declarer will no doubt play a high diamond at Trick 3, ruff out your ace, and play for trumps to be 3-2. He loses control of the hand when they turn out not to be.

If partner has the jack or better in hearts, the defense has good prospects even if declarer has powerful clubs. Hand 4 is such a case. After a third spade, declarer is always down barring a double finesse to pick up your 10-9 of trumps. The defense that wins most often is to cash two spades, play a third spade immediately, and then counter declarer's tactics with the appropriate action.

Finding the right defense on this hand depended on having an exact count in spades. If partner had led the deuce and then played the four, showing exactly four spades, you would have had a different problem. The whole deal:

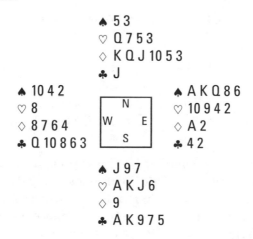

```
              ♠ 5 3
              ♡ Q 7 5 3
              ◇ K Q J 10 5 3
              ♣ J
  ♠ 10 4 2          ┌─────┐          ♠ A K Q 8 6
  ♡ 8               │  N  │          ♡ 10 9 4 2
  ◇ 8 7 6 4       W │     │ E        ◇ A 2
  ♣ Q 10 8 6 3      │  S  │          ♣ 4 2
                    └─────┘
              ♠ J 9 7
              ♡ A K J 6
              ◇ 9
              ♣ A K 9 7 5
```

CASHING OUT

Cashing out is often important at IMPs, especially against high-level doubled contracts. It is always important at matchpoints – whether the contract is a partscore, a game or a slam, doubled or undoubled. Two concepts to keep in mind when a cashout looms are:

- count signals are critical

- look for the suit that can go away

Here are a couple of examples.

    ♠ 5 3
    ♡ Q 8 6 4 3 2
    ◇ —
    ♣ 8 7 5 3 2

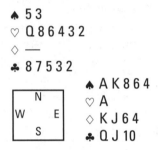

    ♠ A K 8 6 4
    ♡ A
    ◇ K J 6 4
    ♣ Q J 10

WEST	NORTH	EAST	SOUTH
Partner		*You*	
		1♠	2♡
4♠	5♡	5♠	pass
pass	6♡	dbl	all pass

Playing Rusinow-type leads, partner leads the jack of spades. Let's analyze some possible declarer hands.

Hand 1	Hand 2	Hand 3	Hand 4
♠ 9	♠ 9	♠ 9	♠ 9 7
♡ K J 10 9 7 5	♡ K J 10 9 7 5	♡ K J 10 9 7 5	♡ K J 10 7 5
◇ A Q 10 7 5	◇ A Q 7 5	◇ A Q 7 5	◇ A Q 7 5
♣ A	♣ K 9	♣ A 9	♣ A 9

Looking at these examples, it is clearly right to overtake partner's jack and play a second high spade. With Hand 1, the defense then gets the ace of hearts for down one. In Hand 2, the defense is dealt two club tricks but there is no rush to cash them; they cannot disappear. Hand 3 also yields a club, now or later. In Hand 4, the defense can enjoy a second spade only if it is cashed now. The club will still be there, and declarer will be down three.

The whole deal:

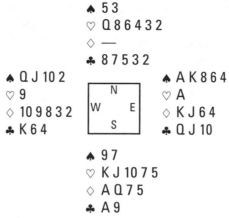

```
                ♠ 5 3
                ♡ Q 8 6 4 3 2
                ◇ —
                ♣ 8 7 5 3 2
  ♠ Q J 10 2               ♠ A K 8 6 4
  ♡ 9           N          ♡ A
  ◇ 10 9 8 3 2  W    E     ◇ K J 6 4
  ♣ K 6 4           S      ♣ Q J 10
                ♠ 9 7
                ♡ K J 10 7 5
                ◇ A Q 7 5
                ♣ A 9
```

The second example of cashing out is a type of situation that occurs frequently at matchpoints. The opponents reach a contract that will be the same at all tables; how do you ensure at least 60% of the matchpoints?

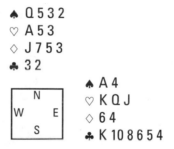

```
                ♠ Q 5 3 2
                ♡ A 5 3
                ◇ J 7 5 3
                ♣ 3 2
                          ♠ A 4
           N              ♡ K Q J
      W         E         ◇ 6 4
           S              ♣ K 10 8 6 5 4
```

WEST	NORTH	EAST	SOUTH
PARTNER		YOU	
			1♠
pass	2♠	3♣	3◇[1]
pass	4♠	all pass	

1.   Help-suit game try.

Partner leads the jack of clubs to declarer's ace. You win the ace of spades, capturing dummy's queen at Trick 2. What next?

Hand 1	Hand 2	Hand 3	Hand 4
♠ K J 10 9 8 7 6	♠ K J 10 8 7	♠ K J 10 8 7 6	♠ K J 10 8 7
♡ 7 6 4	♡ 7 6	♡ 7 6	♡ 7
◇ K Q	◇ A K 9 8 2	◇ A K 8	◇ A K 9 8 2
♣ A	♣ A	♣ A 7	♣ A 7

Chapter 4: What are Defender's Tactics? • **71**

When you study these hands, you realize that clubs is the most likely suit in which a trick can disappear. The exception will be a layout such as Hand 1 where declarer makes four unless you shift to a heart now. But in that case, partner holds four of your suit, a side ace, and a useful-looking void – he would never have passed over the 3◊ bid. You would also have to credit declarer, holding the king-queen doubleton of diamonds, with a psychic help-suit game try. Hand 2 is solid for eleven tricks and the defense does not matter. On Hand 4 the defense is critical. You must cash your club now – hearts are not going anywhere because dummy has too many. Hand 3 has a similar theme, except that after cashing your club, you shift to the king of hearts. Partner will later win the queen of diamonds and return a heart. You set the contract one trick. Obviously, the right play is cashing the club.

Here is the actual deal (Hand 4):

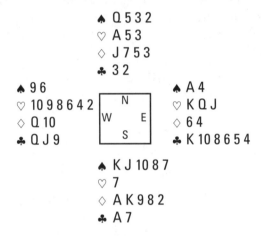

```
              ♠ Q 5 3 2
              ♡ A 5 3
              ◊ J 7 5 3
              ♣ 3 2
   ♠ 9 6                      ♠ A 4
   ♡ 10 9 8 6 4 2    N        ♡ K Q J
   ◊ Q 10        W      E     ◊ 6 4
   ♣ Q J 9           S        ♣ K 10 8 6 5 4
              ♠ K J 10 8 7
              ♡ 7
              ◊ A K 9 8 2
              ♣ A 7
```

STOPPING AN ENDPLAY

Defenders have a few weapons to help fight back when declarer is bent on an endplay. They need to keep in mind these principles:

- do not help declarer in his attempt to strip the hand
- be conscious of which defender needs to be on lead once some suits have disappeared.

Here is a matchpoint problem.

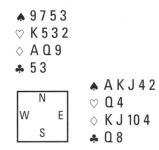

♠ 9 7 5 3
♡ K 5 3 2
◇ A Q 9
♣ 5 3

♠ A K J 4 2
♡ Q 4
◇ K J 10 4
♣ Q 8

WEST	NORTH	EAST	SOUTH
Partner		*You*	
			1♡
pass	3♡	3♠	4♡
all pass			

Partner's lead of the ♠6 is won by your king, as declarer plays the eight. What next?

Hand 1	Hand 2	Hand 3
♠ 8	♠ 8	♠ 8
♡ A 9 8 7 6	♡ A 10 9 8 7 6	♡ A 9 8 7 6
◇ 8 7 5	◇ 8 7 5	◇ 8 7 5
♣ A K 7 6	♣ A K 7	♣ A K J 7

If he has Hand 1, declarer will score five hearts, two clubs and two club ruffs, and the ace of diamonds. As long as you keep a spade for an exit card, he has no way of making an eleventh trick.

If declarer has Hand 2 and you play a second spade, he can ruff, play the ace, king of hearts, ruff another spade, then eliminate clubs, ruff the last spade, and lead a diamond to the nine, endplaying you. If you exit with a club instead of playing a second spade, he cannot strip the hand, and must leave you with an exit card.

Against Hand 3, where declarer needs only one club ruff, declarer can pitch a diamond on a club, lose the diamond finesse, and then ruff his last diamond, making five.

A club return thus holds declarer to ten tricks if he has Hand 2 and costs nothing on the other hands.

This was the deal:

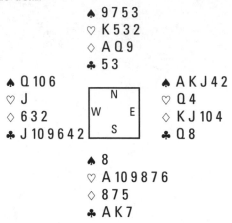

```
              ♠ 9 7 5 3
              ♡ K 5 3 2
              ◇ A Q 9
              ♣ 5 3
♠ Q 10 6                    ♠ A K J 4 2
♡ J              N          ♡ Q 4
◇ 6 3 2       W    E        ◇ K J 10 4
♣ J 10 9 6 4 2    S         ♣ Q 8
              ♠ 8
              ♡ A 10 9 8 7 6
              ◇ 8 7 5
              ♣ A K 7
```

DEFENDING AGAINST A SQUEEZE

In this section, we will look at two examples. The first is a simple squeeze of the type that defenders must constantly guard against, and handle with skill when it does occur. The second is a rarity: a trump squeeze that is of interest because of its elegance.

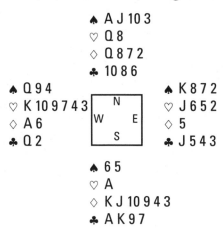

```
              ♠ A J 10 3
              ♡ Q 8
              ◇ Q 8 7 2
              ♣ 10 8 6
♠ Q 9 4                     ♠ K 8 7 2
♡ K 10 9 7 4 3    N         ♡ J 6 5 2
◇ A 6         W    E        ◇ 5
♣ Q 2             S         ♣ J 5 4 3
              ♠ 6 5
              ♡ A
              ◇ K J 10 9 4 3
              ♣ A K 9 7
```

WEST	NORTH	EAST	SOUTH
You		*Partner*	
			1◇
1♡	dbl	3♡[1]	4♣
pass	4◇	pass	5◇
all pass			

1.   Preemptive.

You lead the ♡10. Declarer wins the heart ace and plays the ◇J, which is ducked, and then a spade to dummy's ten and partner's king. Partner returns a low club to declarer's ace and your deuce. You win the ace of diamonds and note that partner discards a heart. Your task now is to work out how to make declarer pay for stretching a partscore hand to a game. What do you play?

It should be fairly clear that you must return a spade. You can count declarer for five diamond tricks, a heart, two spades and two clubs. If he does not have the king of clubs, he is always going down anyway. The danger now is that the conditions for a squeeze are all present. Declarer has lost two tricks; he has ten tricks to take and needs to find one more. If you return a spade, he can take a second finesse now, but his communication to dummy is cut and he must go down. Without the spade switch, partner will be squeezed in the black suits.

If you changed the distribution slightly so that your hand instead of partner's contained the fourth spade, then it is your hand that would be vulnerable to a squeeze in hearts and spades. In that case, you would have the luxury of killing the squeeze either by leading your king of hearts or by playing a spade.

Partner could have saved the day himself on this hand. When he won the spade king, he could have returned a spade to ensure the defeat of the contract. A club return from his side was never important to the defense.

Now here's a much more complex kind of squeeze position. You find yourself defending six spades after this auction:

WEST	NORTH	EAST	SOUTH
You		*Partner*	
		pass	1♠
2♠[1]	4♠	pass	5♡
pass	6♠	all pass	

1. Hearts and a minor.

```
              ♠ 8 6 4 3 2
              ♡ 7 3
              ◇ A 10 6 4 2
              ♣ 9
    ♠ —
    ♡ Q J 10 9 8    ┌───────────┐
    ◇ Q J 9 7 3     │    N      │
    ♣ A Q J      W  │        E  │
                    │    S      │
                    └───────────┘
```

You lead the jack of hearts, partner plays the two, and declarer wins the ace. Declarer cashes the ace, king and queen of spades. Partner follows with the nine, ten, and jack. What have you discarded?

Hand 1	Hand 2	Hand 3	Hand 4
♠ A K Q 7 5	♠ A K Q 7 5	♠ A K Q 7 5	♠ A K Q 7 5
♡ A K 6	♡ A K 6 5 4	♡ A K 6 5 4	♡ A K 6 5 4
◇ K	◇ K	◇ K	◇ K 5
♣ 10 7 5 3	♣ K 10	♣ 8 7	♣ K

With Hand 1, declarer needs to ruff two clubs and a heart in dummy and pitch his last club on the ace of diamonds. He does not fear a heart ruff and would not be playing three rounds of trumps. However, declarer likely has five hearts, from partner's play at Trick 1. He has some hopes for making the hand: a three-suit squeeze (Hand 2); a mistake (Hand 3); or a trump squeeze (Hand 4).

You may only encounter a trump squeeze once in a bridge lifetime; they are not common. When you defend against one, if you recognize it, look for the suit where declarer lacks entries. Thus, with Hand 3, declarer must use a trump for an entry to dummy's diamonds and he cannot ruff them out. One diamond pitch is safe, and you can also pitch two clubs. Now when declarer unblocks the king of diamonds and gives you your club ace, you must lead a heart, not a diamond. A diamond play lets declarer ruff in hand, ruff a club, and now you have no good discard. A heart pitch allows establishment of the fifth heart, and a diamond allows a diamond to be established with one ruff.

If declarer has the guarded king of clubs (Hand 2) he can always make the hand by guessing your now singleton ace of clubs, but you had no defense anyway. One heart pitch or two diamond pitches would be equally fatal.

Hand 4 is always cold for twelve tricks. Declarer has sufficient communication in both red suits to set up the one you unguard. If you pitch three clubs, he makes an overtrick, so when he cashes the king of spades you must unguard a red suit. Your best defense is to pitch two clubs and a diamond. What if declarer's singleton club is a small one instead of the king? Then you could pitch your three clubs and keep all your diamonds and hearts. However, declarer can continue with king, ace, and a diamond, ruffed in hand, and then lead his club. You must pitch a heart on this or the diamonds will be set up with one ruff. Partner will win the club and now has only clubs to lead. When he plays the second club, declarer will ruff in dummy and your pitch of either a diamond or a heart lets declarer establish that suit with one ruff.

This was the deal:

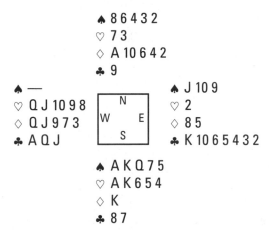

♠ 8 6 4 3 2
♡ 7 3
◇ A 10 6 4 2
♣ 9

♠ —
♡ Q J 10 9 8
◇ Q J 9 7 3
♣ A Q J

♠ J 10 9
♡ 2
◇ 8 5
♣ K 10 6 5 4 3 2

♠ A K Q 7 5
♡ A K 6 5 4
◇ K
♣ 8 7

DEFENDING AGAINST NOTRUMP

SETTING UP DEFENDER'S BEST SUIT

The better you get at defense, the more often you will recognize which rules should be broken.

♠ 10 7
♡ Q J 10
◇ A K 6
♣ J 10 9 5 3

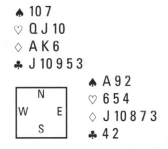

♠ A 9 2
♡ 6 5 4
◇ J 10 8 7 3
♣ 4 2

WEST	NORTH	EAST	SOUTH
PARTNER		*YOU*	
			1NT
pass	3NT	all pass	

Partner leads the ♠3, you win the ♠A and declarer plays the ♠4. Your play.

Hand 1	Hand 2	Hand 3
♠ J 8 5 4	♠ K 8 5 4	♠ Q 8 5 4
♡ A K	♡ A K 8	♡ A K 8
◇ Q 4 2	◇ Q 4 2	◇ Q 4 2
♣ A Q 8 6	♣ A 8 7	♣ A 8 7

If you are defending against Hand 1, no matter how you wriggle, declarer is cold for nine tricks. The defense can take three spades and a club; that is all.

On Hand 2, if you make the conventional return of the spade nine, partner will know your spade holding, but it will do him little good. Declarer will be grateful, however, because he now has the spade suit under control. To give the defense any chance, you must return the spade deuce. Partner will momentarily play you for a two- or four-card initial holding, but he can afford to return another, and your nine removes declarer's stopper and sets up the third spade trick for the defense.

Against Hand 3, declarer is always down as long as you return either of your spades.

On this deal, then, a low spade return is a play that never loses and sometimes gains. That is the essence of solid defense. The actual deal was:

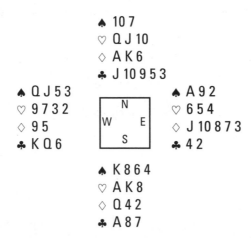

Notice that this play is only advisable when partner has all of the other entries. If you have the ace of clubs, or a red-suit trick, you need to return the nine. Partner can duck if necessary to preserve communication.

The return of your lowest card from an original holding of three cards is most useful when the holding is K9x or A9x. If you started with A10x (and partner KJ9x) or AJx (and partner K109x) the return of the ten or jack collects four tricks. The brilliant return of a low spade might blow a routine defense.

Finally, returning a low card from three is advisable only if you are sure partner started with four. He will no doubt misread the distribution, and if he started with five, that may be fatal.

SWITCHING USEFULLY

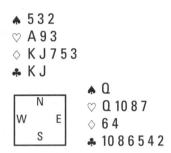

♠ 5 3 2
♡ A 9 3
◇ K J 7 5 3
♣ K J

♠ Q
♡ Q 10 8 7
◇ 6 4
♣ 10 8 6 5 4 2

WEST	NORTH	EAST	SOUTH
Partner		*You*	
	1◇	pass	2NT[1]
pass	3NT	all pass	

1.   12-15 HCP, no four-card major.

Partner leads the ♠J, and your queen holds the trick. Here are three possibilities for declarer's hand:

Hand 1	**Hand 2**	**Hand 3**
♠ A K 6	♠ A 8 6	♠ A 8 6
♡ K J 4	♡ K J 4	♡ J 5 4
◇ Q 9 8 2	◇ Q 9 8 2	◇ Q 10 9 8
♣ 9 7 3	♣ A 7 3	♣ A Q 3

With Hand 1 where declarer has strong spade and heart holdings, the contract is always cold. Partner needed to lead the king of spades to defeat Hand 2. A layout such as Hand 3 is now the only possibility for the defense, so your best bet is a switch to hearts. But which heart? Has to be the ten! Surround the jack in declarer's hand. When you play the ten of hearts, declarer has no good choices. If he covers the ten with his jack, partner will play the king. Declarer must win this and concede one down or else partner will shift back to spades and the defense takes seven tricks. If declarer ducks the ten of hearts, you continue with a low one, and when partner now plays the king, declarer has the same dilemma.

This was the deal:

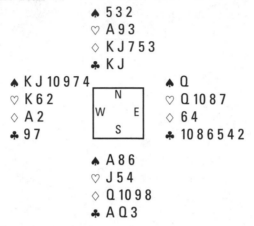

```
            ♠ 5 3 2
            ♡ A 9 3
            ◇ K J 7 5 3
            ♣ K J
♠ K J 10 9 7 4          ♠ Q
♡ K 6 2        N        ♡ Q 10 8 7
◇ A 2      W     E      ◇ 6 4
♣ 9 7          S        ♣ 10 8 6 5 4 2
            ♠ A 8 6
            ♡ J 5 4
            ◇ Q 10 9 8
            ♣ A Q 3
```

Look for surrounding plays with the following holdings:

Q108(xx) with the jack on your left or the nine on your right
K108(xx) with the jack on your left or the nine on your right
KJ9(xx) with the queen on your left or the ten on your right
AQ10(xx) with the king on your left or the jack on your right

Sometimes your only hope is that partner provides the intermediate cards such as the eight, nine, or ten. An added chance is that your play may induce a mistake, because the lead of a broken sequence may confuse declarer (not to mention partner).

BREAKING DECLARER'S COMMUNICATIONS

Two variations of this tactic occur regularly: second hand high and fourth hand hold up. Here are a few examples where an alert defender can play second hand high and disrupt the declarer:

You (West) hold	Dummy (North) holds	Your play
J 6	A K 10 9 4	J
K 6	A Q 10 9 8	K
Q 10 6	A J 9 8 4 2	Q
K 10 6	A J 9 8 4 2	K

These plays often give declarer an impossible guess. Here is a case in point:

♠ A J 9 8 7 3
♡ Q 6 4
◇ 10 9 2
♣ A

♠ K 10 6
♡ 10 9 3 2
◇ Q 6 4
♣ J 4 2

N
W E
S

WEST	NORTH	EAST	SOUTH
You		*Partner*	
	1♠	pass	2♣[1]
pass	2♠	pass	2NT
pass	3NT	pass	4NT
all pass			

1.   Game force.

You lead the ♡9, covered by the queen, king and ace. Declarer leads a low spade. Second hand high here makes life miserable for declarer. If he guesses the spades (dropping partner's doubleton queen), he can make five or six notrump, but give full credit to any declarer who guesses this layout. He's much more likely to assume you have KQx and play low to the jack next time. This was the hand:

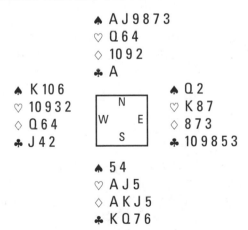

♠ A J 9 8 7 3
♡ Q 6 4
◇ 10 9 2
♣ A

♠ K 10 6
♡ 10 9 3 2
◇ Q 6 4
♣ J 4 2

N
W E
S

♠ Q 2
♡ K 8 7
◇ 8 7 3
♣ 10 9 8 5 3

♠ 5 4
♡ A J 5
◇ A K J 5
♣ K Q 7 6

Holdup plays with an ace are well documented, and there are opportunities with minor honors as well. Look at these next situations.

Dummy holds	You hold (behind dummy)
A K J 10 5	Q 9
A Q J 10 5	K 9

It takes decent nerves to hold up in these situations. Remember also to play the nine from 9x, so that you plant a little doubt in declarer's mind. Always in tempo!

Watch out for these traps, though:

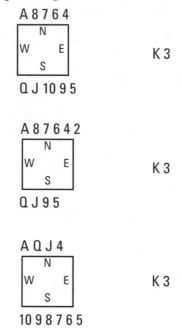

A 8 7 6 4

K 3

Q J 10 9 5

A 8 7 6 4 2

K 3

Q J 9 5

A Q J 4

K 3

10 9 8 7 6 5

In all these cases, declarer will know to drop your now singleton honor if you hold up. Similar risks exist when you hold up a queen. The bidding will often tell you if your play is reasonable.

COUNTERING AN ENDPLAY

The main differences between endplays at notrump and in suit contracts are that at notrump, there is no ruff-sluff consideration, and declarer lacks the option of ruffing to strip a hand. Defenders must still be alert to:

- avoid getting the wrong hand on lead at the wrong time

- lead a suit early to prevent partner's problem

Here is a pretty example from a humble partscore at matchpoints.

```
                  ♠ K J 7
                  ♡ 7 6
                  ◇ K Q J 10
                  ♣ Q 6 5 2
      ♠ 10 9 8 6 2    ┌─────────┐
      ♡ 9 4           │    N    │
      ◇ A 5 4         │ W     E │
      ♣ 9 8 4         │    S    │
                      └─────────┘
```

WEST	NORTH	EAST	SOUTH
You		*Partner*	
		1♡	pass
pass	dbl	pass	1NT
all pass			

You lead the ♡9, partner plays the three, and declarer wins the queen. Declarer continues with three rounds of diamonds as you hold up until the third round is played. Partner follows with the nine and six to the first two diamond plays, and sheds the three of clubs on the third round. After winning the ace of diamonds you mull over some possible hands.

Hand 1	Hand 2	Hand 3	Hand 4
♠ 5 3	♠ 5 3	♠ Q 5 3	♠ Q 4 3
♡ K Q 8 5	♡ A Q 8 5	♡ A Q 8 5	♡ K Q 8 5
◇ 8 7 3 2	◇ 8 7 3	◇ 8 7 3 2	◇ 8 7 3 2
♣ K 10 7	♣ K J 10 7	♣ 10 7	♣ K 7

You know declarer's heart holding is AQ85 or KQ85 – with six hearts, partner could have afforded something bigger than the three. Declarer has a maximum of ten points, otherwise with a double heart stopper he would have invited with 2NT. To justify his opening bid, give partner the ace of spades, the club ace or king and possibly the spade queen. Which is it? The pitch of the two of clubs points towards declarer's having a hand like 1 or 2. If declarer had Hand 3 or Hand 4, partner would have discarded a low spade. Backing your judgement, you lead a spade. You defeat declarer with two spades, three hearts, and the aces of diamonds and clubs. Without the spade shift, declarer could endplay partner for his seventh trick.

This was the layout:

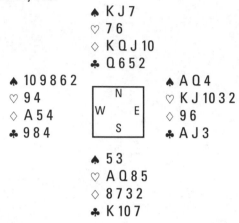

```
              ♠ K J 7
              ♡ 7 6
              ◇ K Q J 10
              ♣ Q 6 5 2
♠ 10 9 8 6 2              ♠ A Q 4
♡ 9 4          N         ♡ K J 10 3 2
◇ A 5 4     W     E      ◇ 9 6
♣ 9 8 4          S       ♣ A J 3
              ♠ 5 3
              ♡ A Q 8 5
              ◇ 8 7 3 2
              ♣ K 10 7
```

DEFENDING AGAINST SQUEEZES

Squeezes, and therefore defenses to them, are not frequently encountered (say once every ten sessions). Serious players want to be able to handle these for bragging rights as much as for their effect on results. A couple of ways to get at the squeezers:

• attack entries to the menace

• do not help declarer to rectify the count.

There are a few 'squeezes without the count' around, but mostly declarer needs to lose all the necessary tricks before pulling off a squeeze.

Here is a little practice in foiling a matchpoint hog (isn't that everyone?):

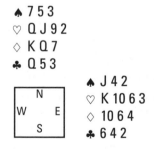

```
              ♠ 7 5 3
              ♡ Q J 9 2
              ◇ K Q 7
              ♣ Q 5 3
                          ♠ J 4 2
                 N        ♡ K 10 6 3
              W     E     ◇ 10 6 4
                 S        ♣ 6 4 2
```

WEST	NORTH	EAST	SOUTH
Partner		*You*	
			2♣
pass	2♦[1]	pass	2♠
pass	3♠	pass	4♣
pass	4♦	pass	4♡
pass	5♡	pass	6NT
all pass			

1. Waiting.

Partner leads the ♡8. Dummy plays low, you play the six and declarer plays the ace. He crosses to dummy with the queen of clubs (partner plays the seven), and leads the queen of hearts. What next?

Hand 1	**Hand 2**	**Hand 3**
♠ A K 9 8 6	♠ A K Q 9 8	♠ A K Q 9 8
♡ A	♡ A	♡ A
♦ A 5 3	♦ A 5 3	♦ A 5 3
♣ A K J 9	♣ A K 9 8	♣ A 10 9 8

Don't worry about Hand 2. Declarer was dealt thirteen tricks, and would have tested spades and played for thirteen tricks via a club break or a heart-club squeeze. Partner could have set Hand 3 by winning the king of clubs and leading a heart to you. Since he didn't, the defense is now doomed: declarer has five spades, two clubs, two hearts, and three diamonds for his twelve tricks. But to beat Hand 1, you must duck the heart queen! If you win the king, and make a neutral return, declarer has the tempo for a squeeze. He can arrange to play all his clubs, then diamonds ending in dummy, leaving you to find a discard on the third diamond; you can take your poison by pitching either your heart guard or your spade trick. But if you duck the queen of hearts, declarer has no recourse. The full deal was:

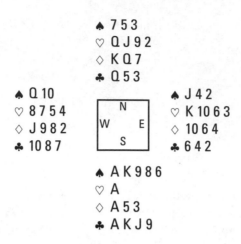

```
              ♠ 7 5 3
              ♡ Q J 9 2
              ◇ K Q 7
              ♣ Q 5 3
♠ Q 10              N         ♠ J 4 2
♡ 8 7 5 4      W       E      ♡ K 10 6 3
◇ J 9 8 2          S         ◇ 10 6 4
♣ 10 8 7                      ♣ 6 4 2
              ♠ A K 9 8 6
              ♡ A
              ◇ A 5 3
              ♣ A K J 9
```

CASHING OUT

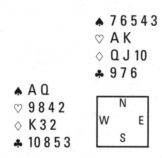

```
              ♠ 7 6 5 4 3
              ♡ A K
              ◇ Q J 10
              ♣ 9 7 6
♠ A Q              N
♡ 9 8 4 2      W       E
◇ K 3 2            S
♣ 10 8 5 3
```

WEST	NORTH	EAST	SOUTH
You		*Partner*	
		pass	1NT
pass	2♡¹	pass	2♠
pass	3NT	all pass	

    1.   Transfer.

You lead the three of clubs, and declarer wins partner's jack with the king. He leads the six of hearts to the ace and partner's five, then leads the queen of diamonds. You win the second diamond after partner has played the seven and eight. Here are some possibilities for declarer.

Hand 1	Hand 2	Hand 3
♠ K J 2	♠ K J	♠ 9 8
♡ J 7 6 3	♡ 7 6 3	♡ Q 10 6
◇ A 6 5 4	◇ A 9 6 5 4	◇ A 9 6 5 4
♣ A K	♣ A K Q	♣ A K Q

In hands with plenty of entries back and forth, Smith signals have priority, and that is the case with this hand. Partner's attitude in diamonds is known and count is irrelevant because declarer has plenty of entries. Therefore, Hand 1 is impossible, because partner could have signaled via Smith that he likes clubs. Hand 2 does not fit for two reasons: the contract is unbreakable, and partner, holding QJ10xx in hearts, would have given you a signal when declarer travelled to dummy's king of hearts. Hand 3 is the one you want, and the ace followed by the queen of spades will pickle declarer. Yes, partner must play the two of spades under the ace (in tempo, I hope) and you continue with the queen for down one. This was the deal:

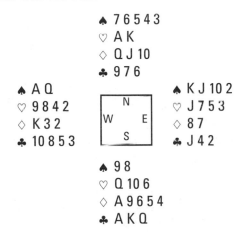

```
                    ♠ 7 6 5 4 3
                    ♡ A K
                    ◇ Q J 10
                    ♣ 9 7 6
     ♠ A Q                          ♠ K J 10 2
     ♡ 9 8 4 2        N             ♡ J 7 5 3
     ◇ K 3 2      W       E         ◇ 8 7
     ♣ 10 8 5 3       S             ♣ J 4 2
                    ♠ 9 8
                    ♡ Q 10 6
                    ◇ A 9 6 5 4
                    ♣ A K Q
```

WAIT FOR YOUR SIGNAL!

You lead the king of hearts (highest honor from a three-card holding) and see the following layout:

```
              ♠ A Q 3
              ♡ 10 7 5 3
              ◇ A K 9 8 5
              ♣ 3
   ♠ J 10 9 8
   ♡ K Q 8        ┌─────────┐
   ◇ Q J 7 2      │    N    │
   ♣ 8 6          │ W     E │
                  │    S    │
                  └─────────┘
```

WEST	NORTH	EAST	SOUTH
You		*Partner*	
			1♣
pass	1◇	pass	1♠
pass	2♡	pass	2NT
pass	3NT	all pass	

Partner plays the six and declarer wins the ace. Declarer then produces the ugly ten of diamonds. You cover, declarer wins the ace, cashes the king, and leads the nine. He has pitched low clubs on the second and third diamond, while partner followed suit. Any matchpoints still available?

Hand 1
♠ K 7 5 2
♡ A 9
◇ 10
♣ A K J 7 5 4

Hand 2
♠ K 7 5 2
♡ A 9
◇ 10
♣ A J 9 7 5 4

Hand 3
♠ K 7 5 2
♡ A 9
◇ 10
♣ A Q 10 7 5 4

If declarer holds Hand 1, you were dealt two heart tricks and one diamond, and you must remember to take them. With Hand 2, you have a club trick coming as well. Hand 3 always contains exactly three tricks for the defense, after you avoided a spade lead. How are you to decide? Duck the third diamond! Wait for partner's signal - partner should know the count of the hand as well as you do. On the fourth diamond, he will play the ten of clubs against Hand 2 and a low club against hands such as 1 or 3. You want to avoid giving declarer a free finesse against Hand 1, where a club shift gives declarer eleven easy tricks.

The actual deal:

```
                    ♠ A Q 3
                    ♡ 10 7 5 3
                    ◇ A K 9 8 5
                    ♣ 3
  ♠ J 10 9 8       ┌─────────┐      ♠ 6 4
  ♡ K Q 8          │    N    │      ♡ J 6 4 2
  ◇ Q J 7 2        │ W     E │      ◇ 6 4 3
  ♣ 8 6            │    S    │      ♣ K Q 10 2
                   └─────────┘
                    ♠ K 7 5 2
                    ♡ A 9
                    ◇ 10
                    ♣ A J 9 7 5 4
```

CHAPTER 5

Counterstrike

The chief thing that the Defending Side must bear in mind is that it is important to try to find out what plan the Declarer is making. After this is discovered, some means should be found, if possible, to circumvent it.

Louis II. Watson, **Play of the Hand**

With a good handle on the tactics available to defenders, you can turn your attention to their application. In many cases, you have a choice of defensive tactics to implement, and you succeed by selecting the one which opposes the direction declarer is taking.

You must diagnose declarer's tactic early enough to take effective action, and some of the most interesting defensive problems are those faced at Trick 1. At this point, you have only the evidence from the bidding, from partner's lead, from the cards in dummy and your own hand. You weigh this information as you try to anticipate declarer's line of play. With good tools and some practice in analyzing the data, just like the weatherman you will become skilful at forecasting events.

On other deals, declarer's intentions become progressively clearer as the play progresses. In a suit contract, the normal play by declarer is to draw trumps. If he does something else, you ask yourself why. Is he setting up a ruff? Why is he setting up a side suit before drawing trumps? In notrump contracts, it is normal to cash a long suit, or to set it up if missing an honor or honors. When declarer embarks on some other approach, you ask why. Is he stealing a trick? Does he need to set up a game-going trick in a side suit because otherwise he will ruin a hand with discards? Can you destroy his communications? Can you cash the setting tricks right now if you win this trick? These are the kinds of questions you must ask yourself in working out what is going on. The table below lists some common declarer tactics and suggestions for defensive countermeasures. Examples follow.

DECLARER'S TACTIC IN SUIT CONTRACT	DEFENDER'S COUNTERMEASURE
Draw trumps	Hold up to complicate matters
Postpone drawing trumps	Lead trumps for him
	Look for the danger he is avoiding
Ruff in dummy	Lead trumps
Ruff in hand (dummy reversal)	Lead trumps
	Look for trump promotion
Cross ruff	Lead trumps
Trump coup	Avoid unnecessary forcing

IN ALL CONTRACTS	
Endplay	Don't help the strip
	Second hand high
	Jettison a high card that may put you on lead
Safety play	Draw the right inference

Work out distribution
Locate high cards
Set up a suit

Avoid unnecessary count signals
Create ambiguity
Hold up a winner: A, K, or Q
Destroy an entry
Sacrifice a trick
Second hand high

Steal a trick
Execute a squeeze

Watch for a ready-made suit
Don't let declarer rectify the count
Kill a menace

Execute a pseudo-squeeze

Signal with discipline

CONTROL AT TRICK 1

Here is a hand in which your diagnosis at Trick 1 gives you an opportunity to pick up some important IMPs. After the following auction, partner leads the ♣3.

WEST	NORTH	EAST	SOUTH
Partner		*You*	
pass	pass	pass	1♣
1♠	dbl	2♠	3♣
pass	4♣	pass	5♣
all pass			

This is the layout you see:

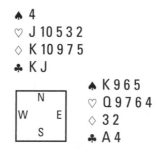

```
        ♠ 4
        ♡ J 10 5 3 2
        ◇ K 10 9 7 5
        ♣ K J
                        ♠ K 9 6 5
              N         ♡ Q 9 7 6 4
        W         E     ◇ 3 2
              S         ♣ A 4
```

Declarer calls for dummy's king, and now the defense is in charge. If declarer has the ace of spades, you will need tricks in the red suits to set the hand, but it is more likely that partner has that card. In this case, you must duck the first trick — then declarer cannot run his side suits without drawing trumps, but if he does so, you can cash your spade winners.

The actual deal is shown at the top of the next page.

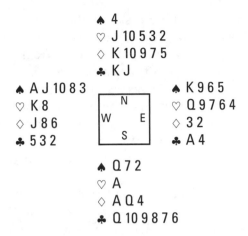

```
              ♠ 4
              ♡ J 10 5 3 2
              ◇ K 10 9 7 5
              ♣ K J
♠ A J 10 8 3          ♠ K 9 6 5
♡ K 8          N      ♡ Q 9 7 6 4
◇ J 8 6      W   E    ◇ 3 2
♣ 5 3 2         S     ♣ A 4
              ♠ Q 7 2
              ♡ A
              ◇ A Q 4
              ♣ Q 10 9 8 7 6
```

Your teammates were in 3♣ making five, for plus 150. After your duck of the ♣A, you are plus 100 and win 6 IMPs. If instead you played ace and another club, declarer made his ambitious contract and you lost 6 IMPs. The swing was 12 IMPs in total. This was a key hand in a seven-board Swiss match, and you ended up with 22 victory points instead of 8. Thank partner for his fine lead.

DECLARER'S TACTIC REVEALS ALL

H ere is a hand from the 1995 World Championship final.

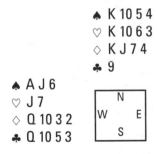

```
              ♠ K 10 5 4
              ♡ K 10 6 3
              ◇ K J 7 4
              ♣ 9
♠ A J 6          N
♡ J 7         W   E
◇ Q 10 3 2      S
♣ Q 10 5 3
```

WEST	NORTH	EAST	SOUTH
You		*Partner*	
	1◇	pass	1♡
pass	2♡	pass	4♡
all pass			

You lead a low club and partner wins the ace and returns the ♣6. You cover the ♣8 with the ten and declarer ruffs. Declarer wins the king of trumps as everyone follows with small cards. He then plays a trump to his nine and your jack. You exit with a diamond; partner plays the five and declarer wins the nine. He cashes the ◇A and then the ♡A. You have reached the turning point. What are you going to discard?

You construct a few possible hands for declarer. He has four hearts, a doubleton diamond, and seven black cards of unknown distribution. He has the king of clubs, and may or may not have the queen of spades.

Hand 1	Hand 2	Hand 3	Hand 4
♠ 3 2	♠ 9 3 2	♠ 9 8 3 2	♠ Q 9 3 2
♡ A 9 4 2	♡ A 9 4 2	♡ A 9 4 2	♡ A 9 4 2
◇ A 9	◇ A 9	◇ A 9	◇ A 9
♣ K 8 7 4 2	♣ K 8 4 2	♣ K 8 2	♣ K 8 2

Partner returned the ♣6 at Trick 2, and you note that declarer could afford the luxury of a safety play in trumps. If he needed club ruffs, he would surely have arranged to ruff two clubs and relied on a 3-2 trump break. You eliminate Hands 1 and 2, and focus on Hands 3 and 4. Obviously you cannot pitch a diamond. In either case you need two spade tricks to beat the hand, and hope that partner has at least the queen of spades or that declarer has ♠Q9 and misguesses the spade position. Consequently, you pitch a club on the ace of hearts.

The whole deal:

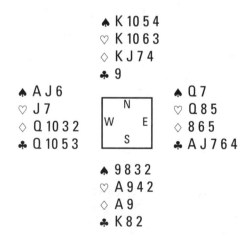

```
              ♠ K 10 5 4
              ♡ K 10 6 3
              ◇ K J 7 4
              ♣ 9
   ♠ A J 6           N          ♠ Q 7
   ♡ J 7        W         E     ♡ Q 8 5
   ◇ Q 10 3 2                   ◇ 8 6 5
   ♣ Q 10 5 3         S         ♣ A J 7 6 4
              ♠ 9 8 3 2
              ♡ A 9 4 2
              ◇ A 9
              ♣ K 8 2
```

Surprisingly, both teams reached four hearts in a World Championship final and the contract made at one table after West pitched a spade.

You must be alert to other, less obvious, tactics by declarer.

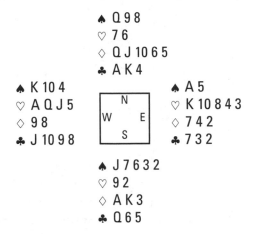

♠ Q 9 8
♡ 7 6
◇ Q J 10 6 5
♣ A K 4

♠ K 10 4
♡ A Q J 5
◇ 9 8
♣ J 10 9 8

♠ A 5
♡ K 10 8 4 3
◇ 7 4 2
♣ 7 3 2

♠ J 7 6 3 2
♡ 9 2
◇ A K 3
♣ Q 6 5

After the bidding dies in three spades, declarer wins West's jack of clubs lead with the king, while East follows with the two and declarer the six. Declarer now leads dummy's seven of hearts, trying to look as though he intends to ruff hearts in dummy, when what he really wants is help in pulling trumps. If the opponents come through with a trump return, he is saved the pain of guessing the location of the trump ten.

This hand poses a difficult problem to the defenders. The key decision must be made at Trick 3, when little information is available. Defenders can deduce from the club lead and signals that there is no future in clubs, and should ask themselves why declarer is neither drawing trumps nor touching diamonds. With the information from count signals in following to the heart suit (East plays the three of hearts), defenders should conclude that a trump lead here will not be productive. No one gets them all right, but your goal must be to up your percentage.

Another tough problem is the situation where declarer has a solid source of tricks and needs to steal a trick in a side suit to make his contract. Again, these problems are much harder when they come early in the play. At Trick 1 or Trick 2, you have much less information than, say, at Trick 8. Look at the deal at the top of the next page, for example.

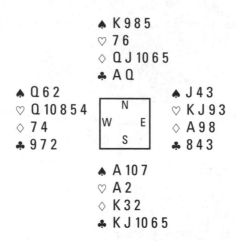

```
            ♠ K 9 8 5
            ♡ 7 6
            ◇ Q J 10 6 5
            ♣ A Q
♠ Q 6 2              ♠ J 4 3
♡ Q 10 8 5 4        ♡ K J 9 3
◇ 7 4               ◇ A 9 8
♣ 9 7 2             ♣ 8 4 3
            ♠ A 10 7
            ♡ A 2
            ◇ K 3 2
            ♣ K J 10 6 5
```

Defending on this deal against 3NT, West leads the ♡5 to East's king and declarer's ace. Declarer crosses to the queen of clubs and leads the queen of diamonds. The reflex action by East is to hold up, but both East and West must be alert to the fact that here, ducking cannot gain — declarer has plenty of entries to dummy. When declarer wins the first lead against a notrump contract, his play often signals that he is either very weak or very strong in the suit led. Here, he took the first heart because allowing a second heart from East would quickly give the show away. With strong hearts and this dummy, he is unlikely to go down.

DECLARER TRIES FOR AN ADDITIONAL CHANCE

You lead the ♣6 (second highest card from a worthless holding against notrump contracts) after this auction.

WEST	NORTH	EAST	SOUTH
You		*Partner*	
	1◇	pass	1♠
pass	2♣	pass	2NT
pass	3NT	all pass	

Dummy follows with the two, partner plays the nine and declarer the king. This layout confronts you.

```
              ♠ 8
              ♡ A K J 5
              ◊ Q J 4 3
              ♣ A 10 8 2
♠ K Q 5 4
♡ 7 6              ┌─────────┐
◊ 10 9 5          │    N    │
♣ 7 6 4 3         │ W     E │
                  │    S    │
                  └─────────┘
```

Declarer next plays the ◊6 to your five, dummy's queen, and partner's king. Partner switches to the jack of spades, declarer ducks; partner continues with the ten of spades and declarer plays low again. How
do you defend?

Here are some possible hands to consider.

Hand 1	**Hand 2**	**Hand 3**
♠ A 7 6 2	♠ 9 7 6 2	♠ A 7 6 2
♡ 10 4 2	♡ Q 10 2	♡ Q 10 2
◊ A 8 7 6	◊ A 7 6	◊ 8 7 6
♣ K 5	♣ K Q 5	♣ K Q 5

You defeat Hand 1 by allowing partner to continue spades. Is this
hand consistent with the bidding? Over opener's two clubs rebid,
responder might have preferred a three diamonds invitation, allowing
three notrump to be played from the North hand, where a heart holding
could be led up to. We will rule this hand out, and give declarer the
queen of hearts.

You can defeat Hand 2 by cashing four spade tricks. But would
declarer really lead a low diamond with this hand where the spade suit
is wide open? He had a great chance for his contract by trying for four
club tricks to go along with four hearts and the ace of diamonds. If four
clubs did not materialize, he could try the diamond finesse for his ninth
trick.

Switch to Hand 3. The point count is right for an invitational
sequence. Why is declarer playing this way? Because he does not know
the clubs are behaving, and can see a possible chance of a diamond trick
if clubs do not come in. You can make him pay for his mistake by overtaking partner's ten of spades and leading your ten of diamonds.

The complete deal was:

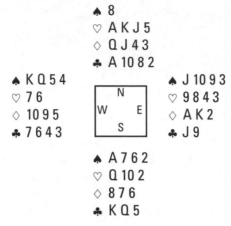

```
                    ♠ 8
                    ♡ A K J 5
                    ◇ Q J 4 3
                    ♣ A 10 8 2
  ♠ K Q 5 4                        ♠ J 10 9 3
  ♡ 7 6            N                ♡ 9 8 4 3
  ◇ 10 9 5      W     E             ◇ A K 2
  ♣ 7 6 4 3         S               ♣ J 9
                    ♠ A 7 6 2
                    ♡ Q 10 2
                    ◇ 8 7 6
                    ♣ K Q 5
```

DEFENSE AGAINST A DUMMY REVERSAL

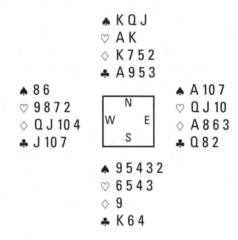

```
                    ♠ K Q J
                    ♡ A K
                    ◇ K 7 5 2
                    ♣ A 9 5 3
  ♠ 8 6                            ♠ A 10 7
  ♡ 9 8 7 2         N               ♡ Q J 10
  ◇ Q J 10 4     W     E            ◇ A 8 6 3
  ♣ J 10 7          S               ♣ Q 8 2
                    ♠ 9 5 4 3 2
                    ♡ 6 5 4 3
                    ◇ 9
                    ♣ K 6 4
```

With no intervention, North opens 2NT, and after a Stayman inquiry, raises South to 4♠. You lead the ◇Q. Declarer plays the two from dummy, partner plays the six and declarer the nine. With this layout, declarer can get home with a dummy reversal unless you take the right countermeasure. He has plenty to do: ruff three diamonds in hand, set up a club trick, and be in dummy at the right time to draw the last trump and cash the good club. This seems like a lot of work, and yet the defenders must be careful not to help: a second diamond lets declarer get home. As West, you have a choice of effective defenses at Trick 2. You can promote partner's spade ten by leading hearts so partner can tap dummy, or you can shift to a trump. Partner must duck this so that who-ever wins a club can continue spades. At that point, playing ace and another trump finishes declarer off.

BLOCK THE TRUMP COUP – DON'T FORCE DECLARER TOO OFTEN!

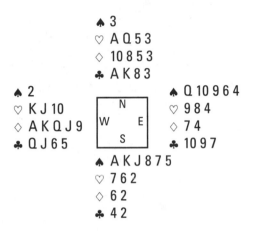

♠ 3
♡ A Q 5 3
◇ 10 8 5 3
♣ A K 8 3

♠ 2
♡ K J 10
◇ A K Q J 9
♣ Q J 6 5

♠ Q 10 9 6 4
♡ 9 8 4
◇ 7 4
♣ 10 9 7

♠ A K J 8 7 5
♡ 7 6 2
◇ 6 2
♣ 4 2

WEST	NORTH	EAST	SOUTH
You		*Partner*	
			2♠
dbl	redbl	pass	pass
3◇	3♠	pass	4♠
pass	pass	dbl	all pass

You lead the ◇K and survey your prospects. Declarer no doubt has six spades and if partner's trumps are broken, he will be vulnerable to a trump coup. If you lead a heart now, declarer lacks the entries to pick up partner's trumps. If you plug away with even one more diamond, declarer can bring home his ugly contract.

DECLARER TRIES TO WORK OUT THE DISTRIBUTION

Defenders should avoid unnecessary count signals and instead construct smoke screens.

```
                    ♠ Q J 4 3
                    ♡ J 10 7 4 2
                    ◇ 6
                    ♣ A Q 4
        ♠ 5 2                       ♠ A 10 8 7
        ♡ K Q          N           ♡ 9 8 6 3
        ◇ 10 8 6 4 3  W   E        ◇ Q 2
        ♣ K 8 7 2         S        ♣ J 10 3
                    ♠ K 9 6
                    ♡ A 5
                    ◇ A K J 9 5
                    ♣ 9 6 5
```

WEST	NORTH	EAST	SOUTH
You		*Partner*	
			1NT
pass	2◇[1]	pass	3◇
pass	3♡	pass	3NT
all pass			

1.   Game-forcing Stayman.

The auction steers you away from a diamond lead, and you lead the two of clubs. Partner's ten wins the first trick and he continues with a club to dummy's queen. Declarer plays a spade to his king and continues with the six to dummy's queen. Here there is no point in giving partner a count signal. You merely help declarer, because partner can infer the count in spades from the way declarer is playing them. Declarer comes off dummy with a diamond to his jack and continues with the nine of spades. Partner can now cash two spades as declarer pitches a diamond, and you pitch one club and a diamond. Partner exits with the queen of diamonds (a card he is known to hold). Declarer can make the hand now by endplaying you to lead from your ten of diamonds. The South player found this play at the other table, but here the defenders have co-operated nicely to create ambiguity, and declarer cannot be blamed for playing for 4-3 diamonds.

DECLARER POSTPONES DRAWING TRUMPS

Defenders should always look for declarer's problem and try to complicate matters. You are East on this layout:

```
                ♠ A K 2
                ♡ 4
                ◇ Q J 9 4 3 2
                ♣ J 10 2
    ♠ 7 4                      ♠ Q 10 3
    ♡ J 8 7 3       N          ♡ A K 6 5 2
    ◇ 10 8      W     E        ◇ A 5
    ♣ Q 9 8 7 6     S          ♣ 5 4 3
                ♠ J 9 8 6 5
                ♡ Q 10 9
                ◇ K 7 6
                ♣ A K
```

WEST	NORTH	EAST	SOUTH
PARTNER		*YOU*	
			1♠
pass	2◇	pass	2NT
pass	3♠	pass	4♠
all pass			

Partner leads the ♣7 to dummy's jack, your three and declarer's king. Declarer continues with a spade to dummy's ace, and leads a diamond, which you duck. Declarer wins the king in hand and continues with a diamond to dummy's queen and your ace. Partner has echoed in diamonds. Declarer is not drawing trumps. Why not? He can only be afraid of hearts. If he holds QJx or better, you cannot get to him. But if partner has as much as the jack of hearts, declarer will surely misguess on the lead of a low heart. Once he does, the defenders are in control. Another heart forces a premature ruff in dummy, and declarer either must lose a second heart, or, if he ruffs two hearts, must give you two spade tricks.

At matchpoints, you might want to cash the ace of hearts first, because the lead of a low heart concedes a costly overtrick if declarer has ♡QJx. You still retain some chances for a set if declarer holds ♡Q109, because he is left with a guess when you continue with a low heart.

MORE ON THE POSTPONEMENT OF DRAWING TRUMPS

Here is another hand where a wily declarer postpones drawing trumps; it comes from the 1985 US team trials.

```
              ♠ A 9 7 3
              ♡ Q J
              ◇ 10 9 7 6 2
              ♣ Q 6
                            ♠ K Q J 5 2
              N             ♡ 10 8 7 6 5
          W       E         ◇ K J
              S             ♣ 5
```

WEST	NORTH	EAST	SOUTH
PARTNER		YOU	
	pass	pass	2♣¹
pass	2◇²	2♠	3♡
3♠	pass	4♠	5♣
dbl	all pass		

1. 11-15 HCP, five or more clubs.
2. Invitational, asking about strength and majors.

Partner leads the ♠8, dummy's ace wins, you play low and declarer follows with the ten. Declarer leads a low diamond from dummy which you win with the king. What next?

Declarer has shown long clubs and a side heart suit. Partner must have exceptional defensive values on this auction, and on this hand that is likely to mean two aces. Here are three possible layouts for declarer.

Hand 1	Hand 2	Hand 3
♠ 10	♠ 10	♠ 10
♡ A K 9 2	♡ A 9 3 2	♡ K 9 4 2
◇ 5 4	◇ 5	◇ 4
♣ A K J 10 4 3	♣ A J 10 9 8 4 3	♣ A K J 7 4 3 2

In Hand 1, declarer can claim eleven tricks (six clubs, four hearts, and the ace of spades). Partner will apologize for his double. Hand 2 is possible, but here declarer has bid a great deal on slim values. Five clubs is down one off the top, and down two if you shift to a trump.

In Hand 3, declarer also has slim values, but a good-looking hand. Why the strange play of a diamond at Trick 2? Declarer's only hope is that the defenders will snooze through the next trick. He is going to trump a heart in dummy, and if he uses spades for transportation, he leaves himself vulnerable to a heart ruff or a trump promotion with a spade lead. If you shift to a trump after winning the king of diamonds, partner can lead a second trump when he is in with the ace of hearts and declarer will be held to ten tricks.

This was the complete deal.

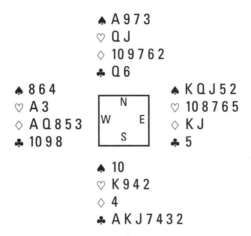

<pre>
              ♠ A 9 7 3
              ♡ Q J
              ◇ 10 9 7 6 2
              ♣ Q 6
  ♠ 8 6 4   ♠ K Q J 5 2
  ♡ A 3   N   ♡ 10 8 7 6 5
  ◇ A Q 8 5 3   W   E   ◇ K J
  ♣ 10 9 8   S   ♣ 5
              ♠ 10
              ♡ K 9 4 2
              ◇ 4
              ♣ A K J 7 4 3 2
</pre>

Note that declarer could prevail by leading a heart to partner's ace at Trick 2, winning the trump return in hand, crossing to the queen of hearts, and leading the nine of spades. You will be forced to win this trick, and declarer can pitch his diamond. Now you have no trump to return and no entry to give partner a later ruff or a trump promotion.

WATCH OUT FOR THE PSEUDO-SQUEEZE

Count signals enable defenders to visualize the situation correctly when declarer is running a long suit.

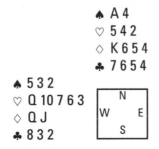

<pre>
              ♠ A 4
              ♡ 5 4 2
              ◇ K 6 5 4
              ♣ 7 6 5 4
  ♠ 5 3 2   N
  ♡ Q 10 7 6 3   W   E
  ◇ Q J   S
  ♣ 8 3 2
</pre>

WEST	NORTH	EAST	SOUTH
You		*PARTNER*	
			2♣
pass	2◊[1]	pass	2♠
pass	3♠	pass	4♣
pass	4◊	pass	4NT
pass	5♣[2]	pass	5NT
pass	6◊	pass	7NT
all pass			

1. Waiting.
2. One or four key cards.

With the West hand, you have a chance to be a hero. You lead the queen of diamonds, partner plays the ten and declarer wins in hand. As declarer runs his six spades, how do you discard? You are going to guard hearts and partner must guard diamonds. Who guards the clubs?

Hand 1	**Hand 2**	**Hand 3**
♠ K Q 9 8 7 6	♠ K Q 9 8 7 6	♠ K Q 9 8 7 6
♡ A K	♡ A K	♡ A K 8
◊ A 3	◊ A 3 2	◊ A 3
♣ A K 9	♣ A K	♣ A K

The defense has no chance against Hand 1. Declarer's ♣AK9 over partner's ♣QJ10 mean that partner alone has to guard clubs and diamonds and a simple squeeze operates.

Defending against Hand 2 the defense is in control. You must be careful not to pitch even one of your lowly clubs, as that would leave partner to take care of both minor-suit menaces. Declarer could set up a criss-cross squeeze and land his ambitious contract. After declarer cashes the ♡AK, he develops this position with his last spade to come:

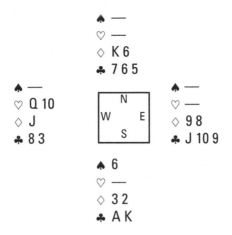

```
              ♠ —
              ♡ —
              ◇ K 6
              ♣ 7 6 5
♠ —                          ♠ —
♡ Q 10    ┌─────────┐        ♡ —
◇ J       │    N    │        ◇ 9 8
♣ 8 3     │ W     E │        ♣ J 10 9
          │    S    │
          └─────────┘
              ♠ 6
              ♡ —
              ◇ 3 2
              ♣ A K
```

On the six of spades (your hand is out of the play now) dummy plays the ◇6 and partner is pickled. A diamond pitch allows declarer to cash the ◇K and return to a high club to make his ◇3. A club discard allows declarer to cash the ♣AK and cross to dummy's ◇K to cash his high club.

Defending against Hand 3, where declarer holds three hearts and two diamonds, you would have to hold hearts and pitch a club. How can you tell the difference? Partner's discards will lead you to the right defense. He will give you a count signal in diamonds at Trick 1, and then show count in hearts as he discards on declarer's spades.

Defending against Hand 2 he will play the ◇10 at trick one, telling you that he has an even number of diamonds, in this case four. Therefore, declarer has a small diamond in his hand which is a potential menace. When spades are run, partner will discard the ♡8 and ♡9, showing three, and you will then know that declarer has two hearts. Therefore the ◇J and your two low hearts are idle cards which you can pitch anytime, saving your three clubs. Declarer must pitch a heart from dummy to retain a club menace, and whenever he crosses to the ◇A, you know to pitch another heart. Of course if declarer pitches two clubs and retains dummy's three hearts, you reverse field and guard your ♡Q.

Against Hand 3, partner will play the ◇2 at Trick 1, and then he will play the ♡J and ♡9 as he follows to spades. You will know that declarer has three hearts, and must be 2-2 in the minors. Both minor-suit menaces are in dummy and partner discards after dummy, so he cannot be squeezed. Your only job is to control hearts and you do not need to worry about guarding clubs.

On this type of deal, signaling is all-important. This is no time for either partner to try a deceptive play. The most helpful plays partner can make are the ten of diamonds at Trick 1, and the eight and nine of hearts in following to the spades. Those plays allow you to visualize an accurate picture of the layout which was as follows:

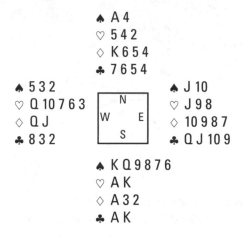

```
                    ♠ A 4
                    ♡ 5 4 2
                    ◇ K 6 5 4
                    ♣ 7 6 5 4
     ♠ 5 3 2                      ♠ J 10
     ♡ Q 10 7 6 3      N          ♡ J 9 8
     ◇ Q J          W     E       ◇ 10 9 8 7
     ♣ 8 3 2           S          ♣ Q J 10 9
                    ♠ K Q 9 8 7 6
                    ♡ A K
                    ◇ A 3 2
                    ♣ A K
```

DECEPTION ON DEFENSE

"The problem here is one of transverse visualization. You gave the opponents a hand to visualize and they managed it with reasonable accuracy. It was in fact the hand they expected you to have, and thus they were able to cope. The hand I had given him to visualize left no room in his partner's hand for any values." Cornelius Coldbottom in 'Cornelius Coldbottom on Deception' **The Best of Frank Vine**, Frank Vine.

Are there any guidelines on when and how to deceive? How can you be sure to fool only the opponents and not partner? Here are a few ideas to consider. On opening lead, there are hands where you can tell that you have all the high card points and partner has a near yarborough. You may try an abnormal lead, such as fifth or third best and hope that declarer misreads the situation.

♠ Q 10 8 7 2 ♡ A 3 2 ◇ A 6 3 ♣ Q 2

You are on lead after 1NT - 3NT. Partner has next to nothing here, and fooling him is of little consequence. Leading the ♠2 when your agreements are 'usually fourth best' may help you against an unwary declarer. You hope for a layout like this:

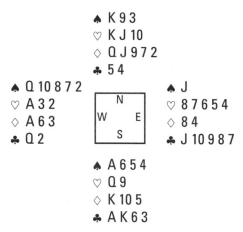

♠ K 9 3
♡ K J 10
◇ Q J 9 7 2
♣ 5 4

♠ Q 10 8 7 2
♡ A 3 2
◇ A 6 3
♣ Q 2

♠ J
♡ 8 7 6 5 4
◇ 8 4
♣ J 10 9 8 7

♠ A 6 5 4
♡ Q 9
◇ K 10 5
♣ A K 6 3

On the lead of the ♠2, declarer sees a danger in a club shift, and may choose to win the first spade. He needs tricks in diamonds and hearts for his contract, and you can use your two entries wisely to foil his plan.

Another case is the situation when you have a wonderful suit with no outside entries and you make an unusual lead in hopes that declarer will neglect to hold up. For instance, holding ♠KQJ92 and no side entries, you are on lead against 3NT. Dummy has implied spades by bidding Stayman, and opener has a hand with no four-card major. A low spade may strike gold if partner has Ax, but that is risky, especially at matchpoints. However, a good shot is the queen (or jack if playing Rusinow type leads).

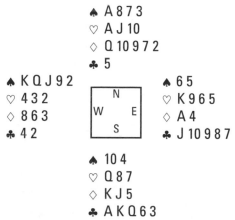

♠ A 8 7 3
♡ A J 10
◇ Q 10 9 7 2
♣ 5

♠ K Q J 9 2
♡ 4 3 2
◇ 8 6 3
♣ 4 2

♠ 6 5
♡ K 9 6 5
◇ A 4
♣ J 10 9 8 7

♠ 10 4
♡ Q 8 7
◇ K J 5
♣ A K Q 6 3

This kind of lead may give declarer a wrong impression about the location of high cards, and should not fool partner. Defending against this 3NT contract, I led the ♠Q (playing standard leads). Declarer won the first trick with dummy's ace and set up the diamonds. Unfortunately, after winning the ace of diamonds, partner failed to think the situation through and returned... the jack of clubs!

CHAPTER 6

Problem Hands

Yes, it is hard work, but that is defense.

Danny Roth, **Signal Success in Bridge**

The following problems come from a variety of sources. Numbers 1 through 19 are from my own experience: tournament play, IMP leagues around Toronto, Canadian team trials, and kitchen bridge games. Problem 20 is from the 1999 US International Team Trials, and problems 21 through 40 are from World Championship play, where one can find plenty of flubs by current, past or future World Champions (all household names!).

Thirty-five of the problems are from IMP games. The other five are matchpoint hands which illustrate typical issues you face in that form of scoring: setting a doubled contract; maximizing your plus against an ambitious partscore; deciding whether to play to prevent overtricks or go for a set.

In the first nineteen hands, declarer play is competent (except for the matchpoint hands), and the bidding is aggressive. In the World Championship hands, you are safe to assume that declarer's play is of the highest order. You cannot say that about the bidding (often very aggressive) or the actual defense that took place. You will notice that many bidding systems are in use: natural bidding, forcing club, Roman club, all kinds of gadgets. Some of the bidding will look downright archaic. The lead and signaling systems are given as they actually occurred, not along the lines I recommended earlier in the book. In all the hands, there is enough information to make the right play (or a very good guess!).

I make the following suggestion to the reader: unless you are truly skilled in the process of reviewing hands in your mind, go through these problems with a pencil and paper. Be prepared for some hard work. I am sure it will be interesting and rewarding. You will learn much more if you take your time, construct possible hands carefully, and work out what you think is the right action before studying the answers. Once you are good at paper analysis, you can take your skills to the table.

Your position as East or West is designated in every case.

PROBLEM ① 1

WEST	NORTH	EAST	SOUTH
You		*Partner*	
		pass	pass
pass	3♣[1]	pass	3NT
all pass			

1.   A rubber bridge player playing IMPs.

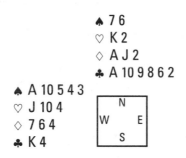

♠ 7 6
♡ K 2
◇ A J 2
♣ A 10 9 8 6 2

♠ A 10 5 4 3
♡ J 10 4
◇ 7 6 4
♣ K 4

You lead the ♠4 to partner's eight and declarer's queen. Declarer leads the queen of clubs, you cover, and dummy's ace wins. Partner wins the third round of clubs with the jack as you pitch a low diamond. Partner returns the nine of spades to declarer's king and your ace. How do you set this one?

SOLUTION TO PROBLEM 1

Hand 1
- ♠ K Q J
- ♡ 9 8 7 6 5
- ◇ K 9 8
- ♣ Q 7

Hand 2
- ♠ K Q J
- ♡ Q 9 8 7
- ◇ 9 8 5 3
- ♣ Q 7

Partner needs either ♡AQx (Hand 1) or ◇KQ10 and ♡A (Hand 2) if the defense is to prevail. Defending against Hand 1, you must switch to a heart; a diamond switch or spade continuation allow declarer to make his contract. Against Hand 2, a diamond shift is necessary to get your five tricks. Which is it?

You play for Hand 1 and switch to the jack of hearts. With Hand 2, partner, holding K-Q-10 of diamonds, would play one high diamond before continuing with a spade. He can work out that declarer has five club tricks, two spades and a diamond. He needs a heart trick to make his contract, and a diamond play from K-Q-10 will never cost, and may be vital.

The actual deal was:

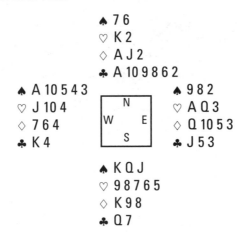

```
                    ♠ 7 6
                    ♡ K 2
                    ◇ A J 2
                    ♣ A 10 9 8 6 2
  ♠ A 10 5 4 3             ♠ 9 8 2
  ♡ J 10 4         N       ♡ A Q 3
  ◇ 7 6 4       W     E    ◇ Q 10 5 3
  ♣ K 4            S       ♣ J 5 3
                    ♠ K Q J
                    ♡ 9 8 7 6 5
                    ◇ K 9 8
                    ♣ Q 7
```

WEST	NORTH	EAST	SOUTH
You		*Partner*	
			1♣[1]
pass	1◇[2]	pass	2♣
pass	2♠	pass	2NT
pass	3NT	all pass	

1. 16+ HCP, artificial.
2. Fewer than 8 HCP.

After this auction, you lead the ♡8 and see the following layout.

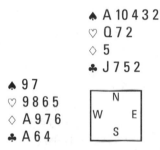

```
              ♠ A 10 4 3 2
              ♡ Q 7 2
              ◇ 5
              ♣ J 7 5 2
  ♠ 9 7
  ♡ 9 8 6 5        N
  ◇ A 9 7 6    W       E
  ♣ A 6 4          S
```

On the heart lead, dummy plays low, partner plays the three, and declarer wins with the ace. Declarer now plays the king, queen, and a low club, and you win the third round. Partner follows to the first club, then subsequently pitches the four of hearts and the eight of diamonds. Ignoring partner for the moment, you shift to the nine of spades. Declarer calls for dummy's ten and partner wins the jack, while declarer follows low. Partner switches to the two of diamonds, declarer plays the king and you win your ace. What do you do now?

SOLUTION TO PROBLEM 2

Declarer has the spade ace, four club tricks and no doubt three hearts for eight tricks. Where will he get his ninth?

Hand 1	Hand 2
♠ 6 5	♠ K 6 5
♡ A K	♡ A K
◇ K J 10 3	◇ K 10 9
♣ K Q 10 9 3	♣ K Q 10 9 3

He has a doubleton spade at most, otherwise he could have raised his partner, so Hand 2 is unlikely. Here, declarer always had nine sure tricks and was trying for an overtrick by ducking the nine of spades.

Against Hand 1, thank partner for her great play of a diamond, setting up an entry to her spade tricks. It is up to you to continue a spade and set the contract. The whole deal was:

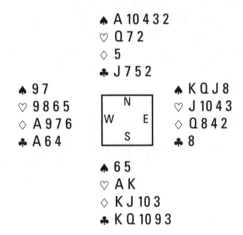

                    ♠ A 10 4 3 2
                    ♡ Q 7 2
                    ◇ 5
                    ♣ J 7 5 2

  ♠ 9 7   ♠ K Q J 8
  ♡ 9 8 6 5   N   ♡ J 10 4 3
  ◇ A 9 7 6   W   E   ◇ Q 8 4 2
  ♣ A 6 4   S   ♣ 8

                    ♠ 6 5
                    ♡ A K
                    ◇ K J 10 3
                    ♣ K Q 10 9 3

WEST	NORTH	EAST	SOUTH
Partner		*You*	
			1♠
pass	2♣	pass	2♡
pass	3♠	pass	4♠
all pass			

```
                ♠ Q 6 2
                ♡ A 6 5
                ◇ K Q 2
                ♣ J 4 3 2
                            ♠ 10 8 4 3
         ┌─────────┐        ♡ 2
         │    N    │        ◇ A 6 5 3
         │ W     E │        ♣ A 10 9 7
         │    S    │
         └─────────┘
```

After the above auction, partner leads the (Rusinow) ♣Q. You signal with the ten spot, and partner continues with the six of clubs to your nine, ruffed by declarer. Declarer cashes the ace and queen of trumps and partner throws the nine of hearts on the second round of spades. Declarer now leads the ace of hearts and a low heart. How do you defend?

SOLUTION TO PROBLEM 3

Hand 1
♠ A K J 7 5
♡ K Q 10 3
♢ J 10 4
♣ 5

Hand 2
♠ A K J 7 5
♡ K Q J 3
♢ 10 8 4
♣ 5

You set declarer in Hand 1 by pitching a diamond on the heart (don't ruff a loser). When you win the ace of diamonds you play another club, forcing declarer to ruff with a spade honor and promoting your ten of spades. Declarer gave up control by playing a low trump to dummy. Two high trumps from hand would have allowed her to take the force with a small spade in hand, and she could later travel to a diamond to draw a third round of trumps.

Defending against Hand 2, ducking the heart also allows the defense to conquer. You can afford to ruff a third round of hearts if declarer leads a high one from her hand. If declarer switches to diamonds, you win your ace and hope that partner has a useful diamond holding such as J9x(x) so that you can take two diamond tricks, a spade and a club. Thank partner for his good lead.

The whole deal was:

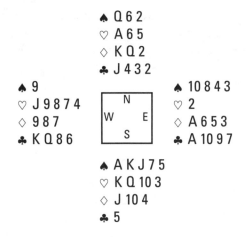

```
                    ♠ Q 6 2
                    ♡ A 6 5
                    ♢ K Q 2
                    ♣ J 4 3 2
   ♠ 9                             ♠ 10 8 4 3
   ♡ J 9 8 7 4        N            ♡ 2
   ♢ 9 8 7        W       E        ♢ A 6 5 3
   ♣ K Q 8 6          S            ♣ A 10 9 7
                    ♠ A K J 7 5
                    ♡ K Q 10 3
                    ♢ J 10 4
                    ♣ 5
```

♠ 7 6
♡ Q 8 6 4
◇ Q J 6 4 3
♣ Q 4

♠ 5 4
♡ K 7
◇ A 8 5 2
♣ 9 7 5 3 2

```
      N
  W       E
      S
```

WEST	NORTH	EAST	SOUTH
You		*Partner*	
		2♡	4♠
all pass			

You lead the ♡K, dummy plays the four, partner the jack, and declarer the nine. What next?

SOLUTION TO PROBLEM 4

Declarer has seven or eight spades here, and a singleton heart. You are playing sound weak two-bids, and this one needs to be very good if you are to have any chance of beating the contract.

Hand 1	Hand 2	Hand 3
♠ A K Q J 10 9 3 2	♠ A K Q J 10 3 2	♠ A K Q J 10 3 2
♡ 9	♡ 9	♡ 9
◇ K 9	◇ K 10 9	◇ K 10
♣ K 8	♣ K 8	♣ K 8 6

With Hand 1, declarer has ten tricks and the defense has no opportunities. Hand 2 will go down if you shift to ace and another diamond now. Hand 3 needs a spade shift and then a spade continuation by partner when he wins the ace of clubs. Which is it to be?

Against Hand 2, partner might well have overtaken your ♡K and led his singleton diamond to get a ruff. He knows that the defense has no future in hearts, and will play you to have either the diamond ace or the spade ace. He will trust that if you had a singleton king of hearts, your diamond suit preference return will guide him to the right play to score down two.

You are left with Hand 3, then. A spade shift prevents a club ruff in dummy. Partner will play a spade when in with the ace of clubs, and you complete a fine defense by holding up one round of diamonds.

The whole deal was:

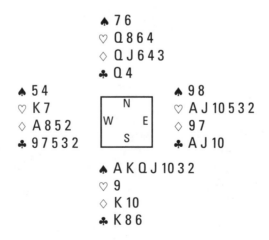

```
                        ♠ 7 6
                        ♡ Q 8 6 4
                        ◇ Q J 6 4 3
                        ♣ Q 4
        ♠ 5 4                         ♠ 9 8
        ♡ K 7          N              ♡ A J 10 5 3 2
        ◇ A 8 5 2   W     E           ◇ 9 7
        ♣ 9 7 5 3 2      S            ♣ A J 10
                        ♠ A K Q J 10 3 2
                        ♡ 9
                        ◇ K 10
                        ♣ K 8 6
```

♠ 3
♡ Q J 10 7 4
◇ A 10 8 4
♣ A 3 2

♠ Q 10 6 5
♡ A 8 6 5
◇ K J 6
♣ 9 7

```
        N
    W       E
        S
```

WEST	NORTH	EAST	SOUTH
You		*Partner*	
	1♡	pass	1♠
pass	2◇	pass	3NT
all pass			

Playing in a matchpoint event, you decide to lead the ◇J against 3NT.
Declarer wins the ace in dummy as partner and declarer follow low. He
then plays dummy's four of hearts to partner's deuce and his own nine.
How do you defend?

SOLUTION TO PROBLEM 5

Declarer has opening bid values or better. You know that partner has the queen of diamonds or declarer would have run the jack to his hand, and that partner has the king of hearts also. Declarer would have unblocked the heart king with a doubleton, and with king-third of hearts declarer would surely have bid game in hearts instead of notrump. The most likely alternatives to choose between are these two:

Hand 1	Hand 2
♠ A K J 9 2	♠ A K J 9
♡ 9 3	♡ 9
◇ 9 3	◇ 9 3
♣ K J 10 4	♣ K Q J 10 5 4

Defending against Hand 1, you can set declarer if you duck the nine of hearts. Declarer has insufficient entries to set up the hearts; he cannot now pick up the club queen, and spades are going to be a disappointment.

Defending against Hand 2, you make declarer a present of an overtrick if you duck the heart.

This decision is a little better than a blind guess. Many players would respond 2♣ with Hand 2, yet one spade makes some sequences smoother. When defending at matchpoints, and you are faced with two equally likely possible layouts, play for the set: you get a better payoff. Play for Hand 1.

The actual layout was:

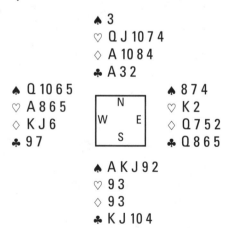

You collect a fine matchpoint score by ducking the heart ace.

Here is another test of your matchpoint defensive skills.

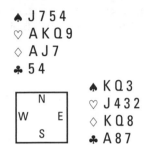

♠ J 7 5 4
♡ A K Q 9
◇ A J 7
♣ 5 4

♠ K Q 3
♡ J 4 3 2
◇ K Q 8
♣ A 8 7

WEST	NORTH	EAST	SOUTH
PARTNER		*YOU*	
		1NT	pass
pass	dbl[1]	pass	2♡
all pass			

1.   Shows the majors.

Partner leads the ◇6, declarer ducks and you win the queen. You lead the seven of clubs to declarer's nine and partner's queen. Partner continues with the ◇4 and declarer wins dummy's ace. Declarer cashes the ace, king and queen of trumps, following twice and then pitching the ♠10 from her hand. Partner follows with the ♡5, ♡7, and ♡8. Declarer now leads dummy's ◇J and you win as partner discards the ♠2. How do you proceed?

SOLUTION TO PROBLEM 6

You expect declarer to have been dealt exactly 2-2 in the major suits with an initial holding of ♠A10. Declarer has preferred hearts with only a small doubleton, pitched the ♠10, and partner has discarded a low spade, showing no interest in that suit. You know the diamond layout exactly and can visualize two possible hands for declarer.

Hand 1	Hand 2
♠ A 10	♠ A 10
♡ 10 6	♡ 10 6
◇ 10 9 5 3 2	◇ 10 9 5 3 2
♣ J 10 9 3	♣ K J 10 9

It is tempting to cash the high trump and lead a spade. You set both Hand 1 and Hand 2 that way, but this is matchpoints and you would like a two-trick set. You do not use suit preference signals in the trump suit, so you must work out the defense all on your own. You have an indication that declarer does not have the king of clubs, since with a doubleton in dummy he might have played the king when you returned a club at Trick 2. Therefore, Hand 1 is more likely. Is there a defense that covers both cases?

Supposing you hang onto your trump for the moment and lead your low spade. Declarer wins that and plays a diamond, pitching dummy's club. You ruff, setting up dummy's trump nine. Now you play the ace of clubs, forcing dummy to ruff. You win the next two spade tricks, and lead your last club. If declarer has Hand 1 he is down two, otherwise down one. You have conceded a trump trick but deprived declarer of two diamond tricks. This was the deal:

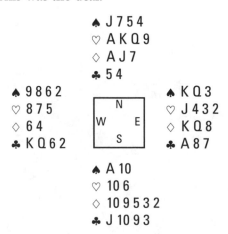

```
                    ♠ J 7 5 4
                    ♡ A K Q 9
                    ◇ A J 7
                    ♣ 5 4
    ♠ 9 8 6 2          N          ♠ K Q 3
    ♡ 8 7 5      W         E      ♡ J 4 3 2
    ◇ 6 4              S          ◇ K Q 8
    ♣ K Q 6 2                     ♣ A 8 7
                    ♠ A 10
                    ♡ 10 6
                    ◇ 10 9 5 3 2
                    ♣ J 10 9 3
```

♠ 3
♡ Q 8 4
◇ 10 9 7 6
♣ K J 9 7 2

♠ A J 2
♡ A J 9 5 3 2
◇ J 2
♣ 10 3

```
      N
  W       E
      S
```

WEST	NORTH	EAST	SOUTH
You		*Partner*	
			1NT
pass	pass	2♠	3♣
4♠	5♣	all pass	

On your lead of the ♠A, partner plays small (count has priority at the five-level). You continue with the jack, declarer ruffs in dummy, and partner plays the ten. Declarer plays two rounds of trumps, ending in dummy, as partner discards spades. Now declarer leads a heart to partner's seven, his king, and your ace. What next?

SOLUTION TO PROBLEM 7

Hand 1
♠ 5 4
♡ K 10
◇ A K 3
♣ A Q 8 6 5 4

Hand 2
♠ 5 4
♡ K 10 6
◇ A K
♣ A Q 8 6 5 4

Partner showed you an original odd number of spades (which you worked out anyway after declarer did not ruff any more). If declarer has Hand 1, you can beat him now by playing the jack of hearts back.

With Hand 2, declarer might have eliminated diamonds before playing hearts. In any case, even if he failed to do that, he has stumbled into the winning line of play. Any heart return concedes a trick to the ten, and on any diamond play declarer can make three diamond tricks.

You must therefore assume Hand 1 and lead the jack of hearts. The whole deal:

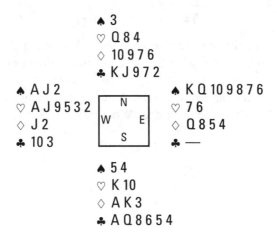

```
              ♠ 3
              ♡ Q 8 4
              ◇ 10 9 7 6
              ♣ K J 9 7 2
  ♠ A J 2            N        ♠ K Q 10 9 8 7 6
  ♡ A J 9 5 3 2  W      E     ♡ 7 6
  ◇ J 2                       ◇ Q 8 5 4
  ♣ 10 3              S       ♣ —
              ♠ 5 4
              ♡ K 10
              ◇ A K 3
              ♣ A Q 8 6 5 4
```

This problem is from a pairs event. You've made a double that you would not consider at IMPs or rubber bridge, but which will garner many matchpoints if your defense is accurate.

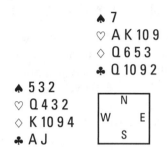

```
                        ♠ 7
                        ♡ A K 10 9
                        ◇ Q 6 5 3
                        ♣ Q 10 9 2
    ♠ 5 3 2          ┌─────────┐
    ♡ Q 4 3 2        │    N    │
    ◇ K 10 9 4       │ W     E │
    ♣ A J            │    S    │
                     └─────────┘
```

The bidding:

WEST	NORTH	EAST	SOUTH
You		*Partner*	
	pass	1♠	pass
2♠	dbl	pass	3♣
dbl	all pass		

You lead the ♠5 to partner's king. Partner returns the ◇7, declarer follows with the eight and you win your king. Time to consider some possibilities.

SOLUTION TO PROBLEM 8

Hand 1	Hand 2	Hand 3	Hand 4
♠ Q 10 8 4	♠ Q 10 8 4	♠ Q 10 8 4	♠ Q 10 8 4
♡ J 6 5	♡ 7 6	♡ 7 6 5	♡ J 6 5
◇ 8	◇ 8 2	◇ A J 8	◇ 8 2
♣ K 8 6 5 4	♣ K 8 6 5 4	♣ 8 6 5 4	♣ K 6 5 4

Partner should have either the ◇AJ or ♣K to go along with his ♠AK(J). He is unlikely to have them all, because that would give him enough values for a game try. You will have a tough time beating this hand if declarer has five trumps. Hand 1, with five trumps and a singleton diamond, cannot be set. You can rule it out anyway because your methods do not allow partner to lead the ◇7 from a holding of AJ72. You are in trouble on Hand 2 also, because partner needed to shift to a trump at Trick 2 to set the contract. Since he didn't, declarer can ruff out the ace of diamonds and set up the queen to go along with four clubs, two spade ruffs in dummy and the ace and king of hearts. On the surface, partner's play of the ◇7 looks like shortness. You think of a hand like Hand 3 and you want to give partner a diamond ruff, giving the defense three trump tricks, a spade, and a diamond for down one. You can also deduce that a spade return sets Hand 3, because declarer cannot run this to partner's ace without setting up a fifth trick for the defense. If he ruffs in dummy, he cannot pick up the jack of trumps and get to his hand to draw the last trump without allowing a diamond ruff. Supposing declarer has Hand 4; now a diamond return allows him to make his contract but a spade sets him.

Therefore, you assume that declarer has four trumps and you return a spade, which sets both Hands 3 and 4. The whole deal:

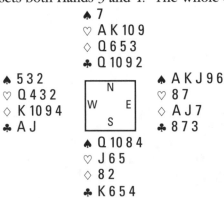

♠ K Q 8 6 3
♡ 4
◇ 9 7 2
♣ K 8 6 2

♠ A 2
♡ K J 10 8 7 2
◇ 10 3
♣ Q 5 4

```
        N
    W       E
        S
```

WEST	NORTH	EAST	SOUTH
You		*Partner*	
			1NT
pass	2♣	pass	2♡
pass	2♠	pass	3♡
pass	3NT	all pass	

You lead the ten of diamonds, and East's queen is allowed to hold. Partner shifts to the three of clubs. You cover declarer's jack with your queen and force dummy's king. Declarer plays a heart to his queen and your king. What next?

SOLUTION TO PROBLEM 9

Hand 1
♠ J 5
♡ A Q 9 5 3
◇ A J 8 6
♣ A J

Hand 2
♠ J 5
♡ A Q 9 5 3
◇ A J 8
♣ A J 10

Declarer drew you a roadmap during the auction – he has five hearts, a doubleton spade, and maximum values for his opening bid. The play at Tricks 1 and 2 tells you that he is surely 3-3 in the minors. He is marked with the A-J-8 (exactly) of diamonds, because with a holding like Hand 1, he would win the first diamond and play one back. Assume then, that you are defending against Hand 2. Partner's club play was an effort to neutralize dummy, and declarer went along with the idea. You can cooperate further by playing your low spade now. This has a devastating effect on declarer's communications; it cuts off a second spade as well as the fourth club. Declarer can wriggle eight tricks, but not nine.

The whole deal:

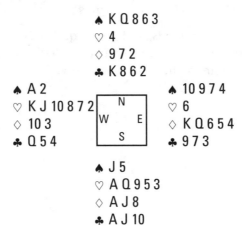

```
                 ♠ K Q 8 6 3
                 ♡ 4
                 ◇ 9 7 2
                 ♣ K 8 6 2
  ♠ A 2                          ♠ 10 9 7 4
  ♡ K J 10 8 7 2      N          ♡ 6
  ◇ 10 3          W       E      ◇ K Q 6 5 4
  ♣ Q 5 4             S          ♣ 9 7 3
                 ♠ J 5
                 ♡ A Q 9 5 3
                 ◇ A J 8
                 ♣ A J 10
```

♠ J 10 8 7 5 4
♡ 3
◇ A 2
♣ A K J 5

<pre>
          ┌─────┐   ♠ A Q 9 2
          │ N │   ♡ Q J 9 4
      W   │   │ E   ◇ K 10 8 4
          │ S │   ♣ Q
          └─────┘
</pre>

WEST	NORTH	EAST	SOUTH
PARTNER		*You*	
		1◇	pass
1♡	dbl	2♡[1]	3♣
4♡	4♠	dbl[2]	pass
pass	5♣	pass	pass
dbl	all pass		

1. Promises four hearts.
2. Maybe you want to take this back?

Partner leads the ◇Q and dummy's ace wins. When declarer calls for a low spade from dummy, you fear a singleton king and win your ace as declarer follows with the six and partner the three. What is the best continuation?

SOLUTION TO PROBLEM 10

Hand 1	Hand 2	Hand 3	Hand 4
♠ 6	♠ 6	♠ 6	♠ 6
♡ K 10 8 7	♡ A 8 2	♡ A 8 7 2	♡ K 8 7
◇ 7 6 3	◇ 7 6 3	◇ 7 6 3	◇ 7 6 3
♣ 10 8 7 6 2	♣ 10 9 8 7 6 2	♣ 10 9 8 7 6	♣ 10 9 8 7 6 2

Partner would have led a spade with a singleton, so you place him with an original holding of ♠K3.

Hand 1 is always down, and on Hand 2, you made a bad double. The critical hands are 3 and 4. Defending against Hand 3, you must force dummy in diamonds before declarer gets the spades going; a heart return lets him make his contract. With Hand 4, you need to get your heart trick in before declarer sets up dummy's spades. Which is it?

Consider partner's two possible hands:

Hand 3	♠ K 3 ♡ K 10 6 5 ◇ Q J 9 5 ♣ 4 3 2
Hand 4	♠ K 3 ♡ A 10 6 5 2 ◇ Q J 9 5 ♣ 4 3

Holding Hand 4, because partner can place you with values in spades, hearts, and diamonds, as well as club shortness, he probably would have continued to 5♡. However, with Hand 3 he has a reasonable double. Backing your judgement, you decide on Hand 3 and continue diamonds to pump dummy. Now the best declarer can do is play for down one. Had you shifted to a heart, declarer could win the ace, play a trump to dummy, ruff out partner's king of spades, draw trump, and set up spades with a ruffing finesse to make his game.

The whole deal:

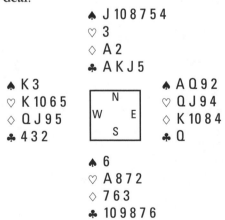

```
                ♠ J 10 8 7 5 4
                ♡ 3
                ◇ A 2
                ♣ A K J 5
    ♠ K 3                        ♠ A Q 9 2
    ♡ K 10 6 5      N            ♡ Q J 9 4
    ◇ Q J 9 5    W     E         ◇ K 10 8 4
    ♣ 4 3 2         S            ♣ Q
                ♠ 6
                ♡ A 8 7 2
                ◇ 7 6 3
                ♣ 10 9 8 7 6
```

♠ Q 10 6 5
♡ 2
◇ Q 8 7 6 3
♣ A 10 6

♠ J 8 7 2
♡ 9 7
◇ A J 2
♣ K 8 7 5

```
      N
  W       E
      S
```

WEST	NORTH	EAST	SOUTH
You		*Partner*	
		2♡	2NT
pass	3♣[1]	pass	3♠
pass	4♠	all pass	

1.   Stayman.

You lead the ♡9 to partner's queen and declarer's ace. Declarer plays ♠A, you and dummy follow low, and partner plays the nine. Declarer continues with the ◇4 to the queen, and a diamond to her nine, and your jack. Partner has followed with the ten and five. What next?

SOLUTION TO PROBLEM 11

Hand 1	Hand 2	Hand 3	Hand 4
♠ A K 4 3	♠ A K 4 3	♠ A K 4 3	♠ A K 4 3
♡ A J 10 8	♡ A J 8 6	♡ A J 8 6	♡ A J 8 6
◇ K 9 4	◇ K 9 4	◇ K 9 4	◇ K 9 4
♣ Q 2	♣ Q 2	♣ J 2	♣ 3 2

If declarer has the queen of clubs you cannot set the hand, so partner needs this card. Defending against Hand 1 or 2, the club suit is frozen, and a club play by you or partner at any point gives declarer her tenth trick.

If you return a heart now, declarer will pitch a diamond from dummy and allow partner to win the trick. Now if partner has the queen, jack of clubs (Hand 4), he can return a club and the defense will take four tricks. If declarer has the jack of clubs and good heart spots (Hand 3) declarer makes her contract. A heart return by partner forces you to ruff and declarer can now draw trumps and set up a diamond for a club pitch. A club return by partner sets up a club for declarer to pitch her diamond.

A club return by you at this point works fine on Hand 4, but allows declarer to pitch her diamond loser on Hand 3.

The line of defense that works against either Hand 3 or Hand 4 is to cash the ace of diamonds and then lead a club. Declarer has no winning options for ten tricks. Say she ducks the club to partner's queen. Partner then forces the dummy with a heart, and your jack of spades stands up as the setting trick.

The whole deal:

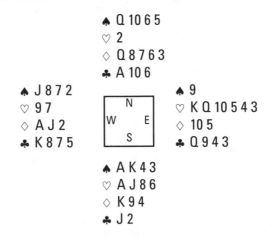

```
                    ♠ Q 10 6 5
                    ♡ 2
                    ◇ Q 8 7 6 3
                    ♣ A 10 6
  ♠ J 8 7 2                          ♠ 9
  ♡ 9 7          ┌──────────┐        ♡ K Q 10 5 4 3
  ◇ A J 2        │ N        │        ◇ 10 5
  ♣ K 8 7 5      │ W      E │        ♣ Q 9 4 3
                 │    S     │
                 └──────────┘
                    ♠ A K 4 3
                    ♡ A J 8 6
                    ◇ K 9 4
                    ♣ J 2
```

♠ 10 8 7
♡ 5
◇ K Q 9 4
♣ A 8 7 6 5

♠ A K J 4 3
♡ K 8 6
◇ 10 3
♣ J 4 2

WEST	NORTH	EAST	SOUTH
You		*Partner*	
			1♡
1♠	dbl	pass	2♠
pass	3♣	pass	3♡
pass	4♡	all pass	

You lead the king of spades, partner plays the two and declarer the five. You continue with the ace, partner plays the nine, and declarer the queen. Can you set this one?

SOLUTION TO PROBLEM 12

You know that declarer has a big hand for his cuebid, and partner has very little. Declarer surely does not have a four-card minor suit on this auction, and that leaves only a small number of possibilities to consider.

Hand 1	Hand 2	Hand 3
♠ Q 5	♠ Q 5	♠ Q 5
♡ A Q J 10 9 7	♡ A Q J 10 9 7	♡ A Q J 10 9
◇ A J 8	◇ J 8	◇ A J 8
♣ Q 9	♣ K Q 9	♣ K Q 9

Hand 1 goes down on a club shift, and Hand 2 goes down on a diamond shift now. But is either one of these hands consistent with declarer's bidding? Declarer's bid of 2♠ should suggest a choice of game contracts, among them 3NT, and both Hands 1 and 2 would have been described by a 3♡ rebid instead of 2♠.

What about Hand 3? Declarer has a powerful, flexible hand, but only five trumps, and if you force him once now and once again when you are in with the king of hearts, you can set up partner's lowly seven of hearts for the setting trick.

The whole deal:

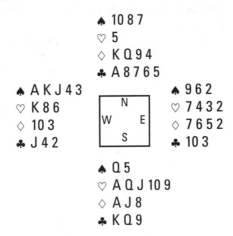

Some players bid a lot. Can you handle them?

WEST	NORTH	EAST	SOUTH
Partner		*You*	
			1♡
pass	2◇	3♣	3♡
pass	3♠	pass	4♡
all pass			

After this auction, partner leads the (Rusinow-type) ♣10 and you see the following layout:

♠ K Q 8 4
♡ 4
◇ A J 8 6 5 2
♣ 5 4

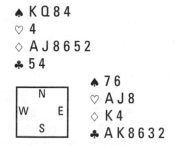

♠ 7 6
♡ A J 8
◇ K 4
♣ A K 8 6 3 2

You win the king and ace of clubs as declarer follows with the five and queen (partner plays the jack at Trick 2 to clarify his count). You continue with a third club knowing that declarer cannot afford to ruff in dummy (that sets up two heart tricks for you). Declarer ruffs with the six of hearts and plays the five of spades to dummy's queen as partner plays the three. He plays dummy's low heart to your eight, his ten, and partner's two. He leads the ♡K now, partner plays the three, a diamond goes from dummy and you win your ace. How do you set the hand?

SOLUTION TO PROBLEM 13

If declarer has seven hearts, he has ten tricks and the defense is helpless. Consider hands with six hearts, where declarer has five heart tricks, the ace of diamonds, and the ace-king-queen of spades for nine sure tricks.

Hand 1	Hand 2	Hand 3
♠ A J 5	♠ A 5 2	♠ A J 5
♡ K Q 10 9 7 5	♡ K Q 10 9 7 5	♡ K Q 10 7 6 5
◇ 10 3	◇ Q 10	◇ Q 10
♣ Q 7	♣ Q 7	♣ Q 7

Defending against Hand 1, you must return your low diamond to set the hand. This cuts off the entry to dummy's fourth spade. The ◇K also cuts communications, but leaves partner open to a squeeze in diamonds and spades. You must retain the diamond control. With a layout such as Hand 2, you must return a spade and eventually win your diamond king. Against Hand 3, the only defense that works is for you to play a fourth round of clubs and promote partner's ♡9. Which is it to be?

Partner's trump plays should help here. He noted your ♡8, and would be alert to the value of the ♡9 holding ♡932. He played up the line in hearts, so you dismiss that possibility, and Hand 3 with it. However, if it is Hand 2, partner's spades originally were ♠J1093, and he would surely not play the ♠3 when declarer plays a spade to dummy with those cards. Hand 1 it is; you bravely lead your low diamond.

Notice that if partner has ♠J1032 and no ◇Q, he cannot signal his spade holding without conceding a trick, and your return of a diamond would hand declarer an impossible game. Life isn't always easy, though.

This was the complete deal:

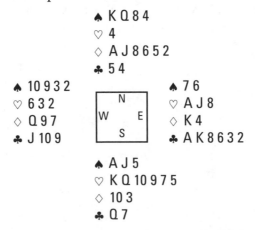

```
                    ♠ K Q 8 4
                    ♡ 4
                    ◇ A J 8 6 5 2
                    ♣ 5 4
    ♠ 10 9 3 2              ♠ 7 6
    ♡ 6 3 2        N        ♡ A J 8
    ◇ Q 9 7     W     E     ◇ K 4
    ♣ J 10 9       S        ♣ A K 8 6 3 2
                    ♠ A J 5
                    ♡ K Q 10 9 7 5
                    ◇ 10 3
                    ♣ Q 7
```

♠ Q 5 3
♡ A K 10 3 2
◇ 10 5
♣ 10 3 2

```
        N
    W       E
        S
```

♠ J 9 8 6 4
♡ 4
◇ Q 6 4 2
♣ A 6 4

The bidding:

WEST	NORTH	EAST	SOUTH
PARTNER		*You*	
		pass	1NT¹
pass	2◇²	pass	2♡
pass	3NT	pass	4♡
all pass			

1. 14-16 HCP.
2. Transfer.

Partner leads the ♠7, dummy's queen wins as you and declarer follow low. Declarer continues with a spade to the ace, a heart to the ace, a spade ruff, and the queen of trumps. How do you defend when declarer next plays the ♣J and partner plays low?

SOLUTION TO PROBLEM 14

Hand 1	Hand 2	Hand 3	Hand 4
♠ A 2	♠ A 2	♠ A 2	♠ A 2
♡ Q 6 5	♡ Q 6 5	♡ Q 6 5	♡ Q 6 5
◇ A 9 7 3	◇ K J 7 3	◇ K 9 7 3	◇ A J 7 3
♣ K Q J 5	♣ K Q J 5	♣ K Q J 5	♣ Q J 8 5

Where are your four tricks on this hand? Partner needs an original holding of four trumps to the jack so that your side has a trump trick, but dummy's ♡K10 warn that partner's trumps are in danger of being swallowed in a trump coup. You also need two clubs and one diamond, or one club and two diamonds. When you mull over the possibilities, you see that Hand 1 could never be set.

With Hand 2, you will require declarer to misguess in diamonds, and you cannot take your club ace too early, or declarer will have two entries to pick up partner's jack of hearts. You must duck the first club, then win either the second or third club and lead a diamond.

With Hand 3 declarer has no hope if you duck clubs twice and then shift to a diamond. Hand 4 requires cooperation from partner. You must both duck the first club, then partner must win the second and shift to a diamond. Your best play, therefore, which covers Hands 2, 3 and 4, is to duck clubs twice. If partner has the king, he should win the second round and his diamond shift will defeat the hand. If you are on lead after the third round of clubs, you make the obvious shift to diamonds and hope for the best. The danger in releasing club controls too early on this hand is twofold: you may either allow a diamond pitch or give declarer the two entries needed for a trump coup.

The whole deal:

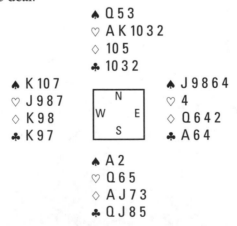

```
              ♠ Q 5 3
              ♡ A K 10 3 2
              ◇ 10 5
              ♣ 10 3 2
♠ K 10 7                    ♠ J 9 8 6 4
♡ J 9 8 7        N          ♡ 4
◇ K 9 8     W       E       ◇ Q 6 4 2
♣ K 9 7         S          ♣ A 6 4
              ♠ A 2
              ♡ Q 6 5
              ◇ A J 7 3
              ♣ Q J 8 5
```

♠ 9 7
♡ A Q 5
◇ 8 6 4 2
♣ A J 8 2

♠ J 10 4 2
♡ 7 3 2
◇ K 10 9
♣ 7 6 5

```
      N
  W       E
      S
```

After a quick auction of 1NT-3NT, you lead the ♠2 to partner's queen and declarer's ace. Declarer plays a heart to dummy's queen, and then plays a diamond to partner's seven, his queen and your king. You lead the jack of spades: partner plays the five, and declarer the six. What next?

SOLUTION TO PROBLEM 15

You consider a few possible hands for declarer.

Hand 1	Hand 2	Hand 3
♠ A K 8 6	♠ A K 8 6	♠ A 6
♡ K J 9 4	♡ K 9 4	♡ K J 9 4
◇ Q J 5	◇ A Q 5	◇ A Q J 5
♣ Q 4	♣ 10 4 3	♣ 10 4 3

With Hand 1, declarer had three spade tricks if he won your jack and returned the suit. In any case, he always makes his contract. If partner had risen with the ◇A and played a spade to you, declarer would have been forced to duck. A club switch by you would then be won by partner's king, but then declarer could safely set up a diamond trick and make his game with four hearts, two clubs, two spades and a diamond.

With Hand 2, declarer again had three spade tricks after winning your jack. He can play on diamonds for nine tricks, or if you shift to a club, he can establish a club for his ninth trick. In Hand 3, declarer won the first spade because ducking would have immediately disclosed his weakness. Partner has played the spade card he would have led back (original fourth best) — the five —under your jack, and hopes that you can read it. Therefore, you must continue spades to take five tricks.

The actual deal was:

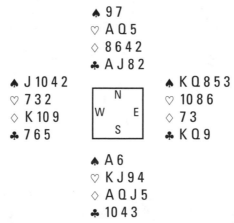

Note that East could safely have clarified the spade holding around the table by overtaking the jack and returning a low one. He can be quite sure that you have not led from ♠J42 because declarer would surely have held up with A106.

WEST	NORTH	EAST	SOUTH
PARTNER		YOU	
		1♡[1]	1NT[2]
pass	2♡[3]	pass	2♠
pass	2NT	pass	3NT
pass	pass	pass[4]	

1. You play four-card majors.
2. A student playing with her guru.
3. Transfer.
4. You wish you were not playing four-card majors.

♠ K Q 9 7 3
♡ 9 2
◇ Q 6 4 3
♣ J 6

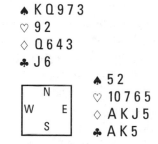

♠ 5 2
♡ 10 7 6 5
◇ A K J 5
♣ A K 5

The opening lead is the ♣3; you win the king and declarer plays the seven. What now?

SOLUTION TO PROBLEM 16

You and your partner have played four-card majors for a while and partner knows how bad the suits can be, especially when you did not double the two hearts transfer bid. Some possible hands for South:

Hand 1	Hand 2	Hand 3
♠ A J	♠ A J	♠ A J
♡ A K Q J 4	♡ A K Q J	♡ A K Q J
◇ 8 7 2	◇ 10 9 8 7 2	◇ 7 2
♣ Q 10 7	♣ Q 7	♣ Q 10 9 8 7

What do you make of the lead? From a worthless holding, your agreement is to lead second highest. Partner would have led the eight against Hand 1. That hand is cold now in any case, and your best defense would be to cash out, sadly. Against Hand 2, you can take six clubs and two diamonds. Delicious! But unfortunately, that hand is not possible: with six clubs to the 10-9-8, partner would have led the nine, not the three.

What about Hand 3? The student can always be counted on to give preference to partner's suit with three trumps, so certainly has a doubleton spade. You can also be sure that she has a full seventeen points to accept her guru's game try. She could have made life tougher for you by dropping the ♣10 at trick one, and no doubt the guru will point this out later. To avoid the guru's derisive laughter, you must find the best way to tackle diamonds.

Partner can hold one of the following diamond combinations:

$$◇ \quad 10 \text{ x} \quad ◇ \quad 10 \text{ x x} \quad ◇ \quad 9 \text{ x x} \quad ◇ \quad 8 \text{ x x}$$

If he has the first holding, you must start with a low diamond. This will also work if partner has the second holding, while with the third, a low diamond will also probably work because the student will no doubt play the eight from 10-8 and partner's nine will force the queen. Against the fourth holding, you must play ace, king and then a low diamond, which is actually right any time declarer has a doubleton diamond. How do you decide? Partner surely has four spades, and likely three hearts, since with four hearts he would probably have led one in spite of the fact that you did not double for the lead. How about the club count? From a bad holding, partner would lead his second-highest card from three or highest from a doubleton. Therefore he must have one of only two possibilities:

$$♣ 4 3 2 \quad or \quad ♣ 3 2$$

He is more likely to have three clubs, since declarer is unlikely to be 2-4-1-6 and have overcalled 1NT. But in any event, since you can place partner with four spades, and at most three hearts, he has to have three diamonds. Therefore ace, king and a low diamond will cover all the diamond possibilities, and that is what you play.

The actual deal was:

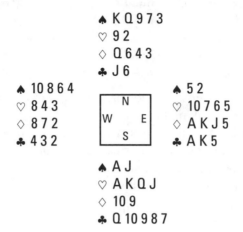

```
                    ♠ K Q 9 7 3
                    ♡ 9 2
                    ◇ Q 6 4 3
                    ♣ J 6
    ♠ 10 8 6 4                      ♠ 5 2
    ♡ 8 4 3          N              ♡ 10 7 6 5
    ◇ 8 7 2       W     E           ◇ A K J 5
    ♣ 4 3 2          S              ♣ A K 5
                    ♠ A J
                    ♡ A K Q J
                    ◇ 10 9
                    ♣ Q 10 9 8 7
```

PROBLEM 17

After the following auction, you (West) lead the queen of hearts. Partner plays the seven and declarer the four.

WEST	NORTH	EAST	SOUTH
You		*Partner*	
		pass	1♣
pass	1◇	pass	1♠
pass	4♠	all pass	

```
                    ♠ A J 10 8
                    ♡ 2
                    ◇ A 6 4 3
                    ♣ J 6 4 3
    ♠ Q 6 4 2
    ♡ K Q 10 8       N
    ◇ 9 8 5       W     E
    ♣ K 8            S
```

You have a heart trick in and a sure club trick on the horizon. Partner needs a trick or two to help out.

SOLUTION TO PROBLEM 17

Hand 1	Hand 2	Hand 3
♠ K 9 7 3	♠ K 9 7 3	♠ K 9 7 3
♡ J 9 4	♡ J 9 4	♡ J 9 4
◇ K 2	◇ K Q	◇ Q 2
♣ A Q 10 7	♣ A 9 7 2	♣ A Q 7 2

Against Hand 1, the defense cannot prevent declarer from ruffing two hearts in dummy and making his game.

Against Hand 2 the defense has two club tricks to go along with a heart. Continuing hearts ensures a trick for the queen of spades.

The same theme applies against Hand 3. There is no rush to set up your diamond trick. A heart it is. This was the deal:

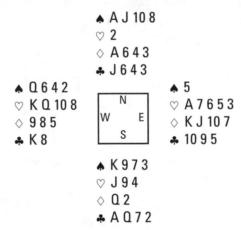

```
                    ♠ A J 10 8
                    ♡ 2
                    ◇ A 6 4 3
                    ♣ J 6 4 3
   ♠ Q 6 4 2                        ♠ 5
   ♡ K Q 10 8         N             ♡ A 7 6 5 3
   ◇ 9 8 5        W        E        ◇ K J 10 7
   ♣ K 8              S             ♣ 10 9 5
                    ♠ K 9 7 3
                    ♡ J 9 4
                    ◇ Q 2
                    ♣ A Q 7 2
```

Partner leads the ♠9 after this auction:

WEST	NORTH	EAST	SOUTH
Partner		*You*	
	1♣[1]	1♠	2♣[2]
pass	3♣	pass	3NT
all pass			

1. 16+ HCP.
2. Natural, game force.

Dummy follows with the three, you win the king and declarer follows with the eight. This layout confronts you:

> ♠ 3
> ♡ Q 9 5 4
> ◇ A K 8
> ♣ A Q J 10 6

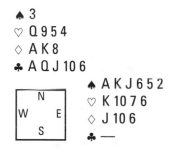

> ♠ A K J 6 5 2
> ♡ K 10 7 6
> ◇ J 10 6
> ♣ —

Your partnership agreement is to lead low with three small in a suit you have not supported, so you know that you must not cash another spade. Your jack of diamonds holds the next trick, as declarer plays the seven and partner the four. You continue a diamond: declarer plays the nine and partner the two as dummy's ace wins. You can see five rounds of clubs coming. How do you plan your discards?

SOLUTION TO PROBLEM 18

Declarer must have the ace of hearts, queen of spades, and king of clubs for his bid. There are two possible hands to consider.

Hand 1	Hand 2
♠ Q 10 8 4	♠ Q 10 8 4
♡ A 2	♡ A
◇ 9 7	◇ 9 7 5
♣ K 5 4 3 2	♣ K 5 4 3 2

Declarer has promised five-plus clubs, and if he has six, he has nine tricks. So, you must give him either a doubleton heart and a doubleton diamond (Hand 1) or a singleton ♡A and three diamonds (Hand 2).

Against Hand 1, the defense is helpless. Declarer can always arrive at a four-card ending where you must come down to

♠ A J ♡ K 10 ◇ — ♣ —

Had you bared either of your honors, declarer would have an easy ninth trick. Now, however, he can endplay you by either playing ace and another heart or exiting with a high spade.

A major clue comes from the diamond spot cards. Your agreement with partner is to signal with the highest affordable card. Partner's first signal was with the four of diamonds, so declarer likely has the nine, seven and five. His distribution looks like 4-1-3-5. This thought leads you to Hand 2. Here you must keep three hearts and two spades. Declarer will cash his clubs, cash the ♡A, travel to dummy with a diamond and play a low heart. If your ♡K is now bare, you will be forced to give declarer a ninth trick in spades. If you have foreseen the position and kept a small heart, you can duck this trick to partner's jack. Partner will cash his last diamond, and you take the last two tricks with the king of hearts and ace of spades.

The complete deal was:

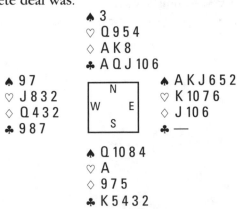

Playing matchpoints, you hear this bidding:

WEST	NORTH	EAST	SOUTH
Partner		*You*	
		pass	3♡
dbl	all pass		

♠ A Q 9 6 5
♡ —
◇ K 6 5 4
♣ A Q 10 3

♠ J 10
♡ K Q 10 9 2
◇ Q J 7 3
♣ 9 2

```
      N
   W     E
      S
```

The auction filled you with a feeling of great anticipation, but that all changed when partner led the five of clubs and you saw the strength of the dummy. Partner has added new meaning to the old saw that 'the partner with shape is the one who must act over preempts.' Declarer wins with the club jack and plays ace and another heart. Partner discards the ten of diamonds on the second heart. Can you see five tricks from the East seat?

SOLUTION TO PROBLEM 19

You mull over some possibilities and consider these hands for South:

Hand 1	Hand 2	Hand 3
♠ 8 7	♠ 8 7	♠ 8 7
♡ A J 8 7 6 5 4	♡ A J 8 7 6 5 4	♡ A J 8 7 6 5 4
◇ —	◇ 8 2	◇ 2
♣ J 8 6 4	♣ J 8	♣ J 8 4

You know declarer's exact heart holding. How about the other cards? If he has Hand 1, you cannot set declarer. The defense gets four heart tricks and that is all.

Defending against Hand 2, a club or spade return will do the job. Partner must have four spades to double with so few high cards, and a spade return gives declarer a finesse he was going to take anyway. Now if declarer plays ace and another spade, you can pitch your club and guarantee a fifth trick. Similarly, if declarer tries ace and a low club, you can pitch your last spade. Declarer cannot come off dummy by playing diamonds, because that obviously gives the defense two diamond tricks and a sure two-trick set. Hand 3 is really the layout you expect from the auction, where partner has perfect shape for his light double. A spade return to the queen forces declarer either to play ace and another spade (on which you will pitch your remaining club) or to exit with a low diamond, when you will win your jack and play a second spade. The defensive trap to avoid on this hand is that of obeying partner's signal of the ◇10. Partner does not really want a diamond lead; he is just confirming that he has the ace.

The whole deal was:

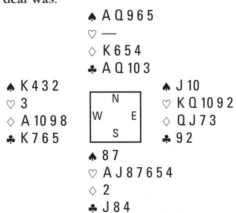

```
                  ♠ A Q 9 6 5
                  ♡ —
                  ◇ K 6 5 4
                  ♣ A Q 10 3
      ♠ K 4 3 2         N        ♠ J 10
      ♡ 3                        ♡ K Q 10 9 2
      ◇ A 10 9 8   W       E     ◇ Q J 7 3
      ♣ K 7 6 5         S        ♣ 9 2
                  ♠ 8 7
                  ♡ A J 8 7 6 5 4
                  ◇ 2
                  ♣ J 8 4
```

Declarer could succeed with a diamond play at Trick 2, pitching his third club and using his entries to ruff diamonds and execute a trump coup.

♠ A J
♡ 7 5
◇ A J 4 2
♣ 10 9 8 4 2

```
        ♠ 6 3
   N    ♡ K 9 4 2
W    E  ◇ 8 6 3
   S    ♣ Q J 7 6
```

WEST	NORTH	EAST	SOUTH
Partner		*You*	
1◇¹	pass	1♡	pass
2♡	pass	pass	2♠
all pass			

1. Playing weak notrumps.

Partner (West) leads the ace of hearts. He follows with the queen and then the three of hearts, ruffed in dummy. Declarer cashes the ace of spades and leads dummy's ten of clubs. You cover with the jack, declarer plays the king and partner the ace. You win the club return with the queen. What should you play next?

SOLUTION TO PROBLEM 20

Partner's hand resembles a strong notrump. He led an ace lacking the king so he did not have an attractive holding in another suit to lead, and he probably has four hearts for his immediate raise. Partner wanted to force dummy so he may (but not for sure) have interesting trump spots. Since he chose not to overcall immediately, declarer has an indifferent hand with five or six spades. Here are some possible hands.

Hand 1	Hand 2	Hand 3	Hand 4	Hand 5
♠ K 10 9 5 4 2	♠ Q 10 9 5 4 2	♠ Q 10 9 8 4	♠ K 10 9 8 7	♠ K 10 9 5 4
♡ 10 8 6	♡ 10 8 6	♡ 10 8 6	♡ J 10 8 6	♡ 10 8 6
◇ Q 10	◇ Q 10	◇ Q 10 9	◇ Q 10	◇ Q 10 9
♣ K 5	♣ K 5	♣ K 5	♣ K 5	♣ K 5

Hands 1 and 2 are cold: declarer gets a heart ruff, five spades and two diamonds. If declarer has six trumps, partner needs the nine or ten of spades along with the king; then a club will promote the setting trick.

Hand 3 is dangerous because declarer may make four spades, a ruff, and three diamonds. However, a club lead now lets partner pitch a diamond, and he will then have the option of ruffing a diamond, or if declarer tries to draw trumps, of forcing declarer with his last heart to develop the setting trick. A club return also sets Hand 5; partner pitches a diamond if declarer ruffs high, or overruffs if declarer ruffs low. It looks like a heart is needed to set Hand 4, but in fact, a club return will set Hand 4 as well. Partner will overruff declarer and return the ◇K. This leaves declarer with a losing heart. So a club it is.

In the final of the 1999 US International Team Trials, East returned a heart, allowing the contract to make for a 5-IMP loss. The whole deal was:

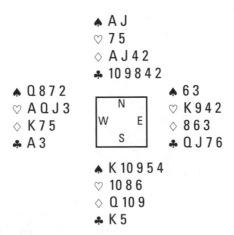

```
            ♠ A J
            ♡ 7 5
            ◇ A J 4 2
            ♣ 10 9 8 4 2
♠ Q 8 7 2        N        ♠ 6 3
♡ A Q J 3    W       E    ♡ K 9 4 2
◇ K 7 5          S        ◇ 8 6 3
♣ A 3                     ♣ Q J 7 6
            ♠ K 10 9 5 4
            ♡ 10 8 6
            ◇ Q 10 9
            ♣ K 5
```

PROBLEM 21

♠ A 7
♡ 5
◇ K 10 7 2
♣ A Q J 8 3 2

                    ♠ Q J 10 6
                    ♡ K J 9 7
                    ◇ J 6 5
                    ♣ K 9

WEST	NORTH	EAST	SOUTH
PARTNER		*You*	
pass	2♣ [1]	pass	2NT
pass	3NT	all pass	

1. 11-15 HCP, clubs.

Partner leads the ♠2 to your ten and declarer's king. Declarer plays a
club to dummy's jack as partner follows with the four. What now?

SOLUTION TO PROBLEM 21

Hand 1	Hand 2	Hand 3	Hand 4
♠ K 8 4	♠ K 8 4	♠ K 8 4	♠ K 8 4
♡ Q 10 6 2	♡ Q 8 6 2	♡ 10 8 6 2	♡ Q 8 6 2
◇ A 9 4 3	◇ A 9 4 3	◇ A Q 4 3	◇ A Q
♣ 6 5	♣ 6 5	♣ 6 5	♣ 10 7 6 5

Partner chose to lead a bad four-card suit, so you can assume he has no five-card suit, and therefore he has four hearts at most. Declarer probably has no more than four hearts because he did not make an inquiry about a major-suit contract. The key cards on this hand are the ♡ A,Q,10, and the ◇ A. If declarer has the ♡ A and ◇ A, or the ♡ AQ, he is cold. If he has as much as ♡ Q10xx, partner needs the ace of diamonds to set the hand. For instance, Hand 1 is cold.

There is no point in ducking the club (and it's embarrassing if declarer has Hand 4). The return of the ♡ J or ♡ 9 sets Hands 2, 3, and 4, and since the jack is easiest to read, that is what you should play.

The whole deal:

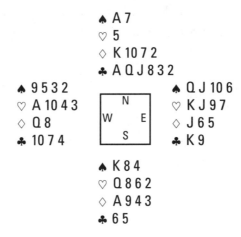

In the 1971 World Championship Round Robin, the declarer for the Aces scored plus 460 against less than perfect Australian defense.

♠ 8
♡ 6 4 2
◇ Q 10 9 6
♣ A K J 7 5

```
        N
  W         E
        S
```

♠ 10 2
♡ A Q 10 5
◇ K 5 4
♣ Q 8 6 2

WEST	NORTH	EAST	SOUTH
PARTNER		*YOU*	
1♠	2♣	dbl¹	pass
pass	redbl	pass	2NT
pass	pass	dbl	all pass

1. Penalty.

Partner leads the ♠5, and your ten loses to the queen. Declarer leads the ♣4, partner discards the ♠3, declarer plays dummy's jack, and you win the queen. What now?

SOLUTION TO PROBLEM 22

Four hands should cover the main possibilities:

Hand 1	Hand 2	Hand 3	Hand 4
♠ K Q 7 6	♠ K Q 7 6	♠ K Q J 6	♠ K Q J 9
♡ K J 7	♡ K 7	♡ J 7	♡ K 7
◇ J 2	◇ 7 3 2	◇ J 7 2	◇ 7 3 2
♣ 10 9 4 3	♣ 10 9 4 3	♣ 10 9 4 3	♣ 10 9 4 3

From partner's spade discard, you know that he does not have an overwhelming suit, although he probably started with six of them. If declarer's hand is 1 or 2, partner would have pitched a heart or a diamond, not a spade. You focus on Hands 3 and 4 to work out your continuation. A spade return sets Hand 3, but if partner then continues spades, declarer is down only two. If you are defending Hand 4, a spade return lets declarer make his contract!

The clues point to a heart switch. That play ensures a set against Hand 4, and produces a three-trick penalty against Hand 3.

The whole deal:

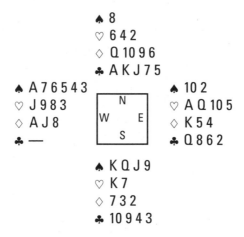

```
              ♠ 8
              ♡ 6 4 2
              ◇ Q 10 9 6
              ♣ A K J 7 5
 ♠ A 7 6 5 4 3            ♠ 10 2
 ♡ J 9 8 3       N       ♡ A Q 10 5
 ◇ A J 8     W     E     ◇ K 5 4
 ♣ —             S       ♣ Q 8 6 2
              ♠ K Q J 9
              ♡ K 7
              ◇ 7 3 2
              ♣ 10 9 4 3
```

In the 1971 World Championship Round Robin, the Australian declarer made 2NT doubled when the North American defender returned a spade after winning the club queen.

♠ J 10 9 6
♡ 10 9 6 3
◇ K Q 7
♣ A 2

♠ K 8 7 5 4
♡ Q 4
◇ 10 8
♣ Q 10 7 6

```
    N
W       E
    S
```

WEST	NORTH	EAST	SOUTH
You		*Partner*	
			1NT
pass	2♣	pass	2NT[1]
pass	3NT	all pass	

1.   15-16 HCP, no four-card major.

You lead the ♠5 to dummy's nine, partner's queen and declarer's ace. Declarer leads a diamond to dummy's queen and partner's two. When declarer leads the ♠J from dummy, partner plays the ♣3, and declarer the ♠2. Your turn.

SOLUTION TO PROBLEM 23

A survey of points around the table tells you that if partner has both the ace and king of hearts, declarer is left with at most fourteen points for his bid. You also see that if partner has the ace or king-jack of hearts, declarer must have the ace of diamonds and king of clubs, and an easy nine tricks. You therefore assign the ace and king of hearts to declarer in considering your options.

Hand 1	Hand 2	Hand 3	Hand 4
♠ A 3 2	♠ A 3 2	♠ A 3 2	♠ A 3 2
♡ A K J	♡ A K 8	♡ A K 8	♡ A K J
◇ A 9 6 5	◇ J 9 6 5 3	◇ 6 5 3	◇ 9 6 5 4 3
♣ 9 6 4	♣ K J	♣ K J 5 4	♣ K J

Holding Hand 1, declarer had ten tricks by returning a spade at Trick 2 instead of crossing to dummy. With Hand 2, declarer would just continue diamonds to land his contract. He has ten or eleven tricks in any case. With Hand 3, declarer jeopardizes the contract by playing diamonds at Trick 2; likewise partner, with ◇AJxxx, would have played a higher diamond than the two.

This analysis leads you to Hand 4, which you can set by winning the spade now, and shifting to a club. What about partner's discouraging club? Does he have four? Probably not, as declarer would have a singleton heart. So, partner surely had five clubs initially.

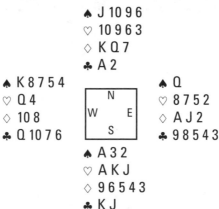

```
              ♠ J 10 9 6
              ♡ 10 9 6 3
              ◇ K Q 7
              ♣ A 2
♠ K 8 7 5 4                    ♠ Q
♡ Q 4          N               ♡ 8 7 5 2
◇ 10 8       W   E             ◇ A J 2
♣ Q 10 7 6     S              ♣ 9 8 5 4 3
              ♠ A 3 2
              ♡ A K J
              ◇ 9 6 5 4 3
              ♣ K J
```

In the 1971 World Championship, the North American declarer made 3NT when West shifted to the ♡Q at Trick 4. At the other table, the Australian declarer was plus 660 after returning a spade at Trick 2, a play which presented the defense with a much more difficult problem.

♠ A Q 8 6 4
♡ 8 7 6 3
◇ 7 6 5 3
♣ —

♠ K 9 7 3
♡ 9 5
◇ A J 4 2
♣ K 8 5

```
  N
W   E
  S
```

WEST	NORTH	EAST	SOUTH
You		*Partner*	
pass	pass	pass	1◇
pass	1♠	5♣	dbl
pass	5◇	pass	pass
dbl	all pass		

You lead the ♣5 and it is ruffed in dummy as partner plays the two and declarer the jack. Declarer plays dummy's ◇5, partner pitches the ♣10, and declarer plays the queen. What next?

SOLUTION TO PROBLEM 24

Hand 1
♠ J 5 2
♡ A K J 5
◇ K Q 10 9 8
♣ J

Hand 2
♠ J 5 2
♡ A K 5 4
◇ K Q 10 9 8
♣ J

Hand 3
♠ J 10 2
♡ A Q 5 4
◇ K Q 10 9 8
♣ J

Partner is showing an odd number of clubs - nine! You know the club and diamond positions, and need only work out the key spade and heart possibilities. If declarer has Hand 1 (or ♡AQJx) he can always make eleven tricks. Partner's hearts must be as good as QJ10 or KJ10 to set this hand, and the dangerous spade suit must be neutralized. You assign declarer a hand such as 2 or 3, and start your campaign by duck-ing the first diamond. Now, if he continues diamonds, you win and play a heart. Then win the next diamond and play another heart. Declarer now does not have enough entries to use the spades. You cover the sec-ond spade, of course, not the first.

If declarer starts spades (you don't cover) after the first diamond is ducked, and then reverts to diamonds, you will win and play another spade yourself. Then on winning the next diamond, you play king of spades, killing dummy while you still have a trump.

The whole deal:

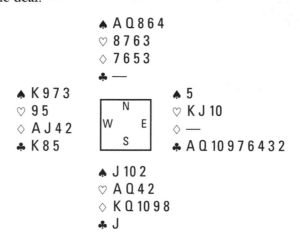

♠ A Q 8 6 4
♡ 8 7 6 3
◇ 7 6 5 3
♣ —

♠ K 9 7 3
♡ 9 5
◇ A J 4 2
♣ K 8 5

♠ 5
♡ K J 10
◇ —
♣ A Q 10 9 7 6 4 3 2

♠ J 10 2
♡ A Q 4 2
◇ K Q 10 9 8
♣ J

In the 1971 World Championship Round Robin, the Chinese declarer was plus 750 against Brazil.

♠ 6 4
♡ K 2
◇ A 8 6 5
♣ A K J 7 2

♠ A J 10 7 2
♡ A Q J 9 8
◇ J 7
♣ 9

```
        N
    W       E
        S
```

WEST	NORTH	EAST	SOUTH
You		*Partner*	
1♠	2♣	pass	2NT
pass	3NT	all pass	

You lead the ♡Q to dummy's king, partner's seven and declarer's three. A diamond from dummy elicits partner's four and declarer's nine as you win the jack. What next?

SOLUTION TO PROBLEM 25

Hand 1	Hand 2	Hand 3	Hand 4
♠ K 8 3	♠ K 8 5 3	♠ Q 8 5	♠ K 8 3
♡ 10 5 4 3	♡ 10 3	♡ 10 5 4 3	♡ 10 5 4 3
◇ K 9 3 2	◇ K 9 3 2	◇ K 9 3 2	◇ K 9 3
♣ Q 10	♣ Q 10 5	♣ Q 10	♣ Q 5 4

Right now, you wish you had led a spade. Partner has the king or queen (if declarer had the king-queen of spades he would have played one at Trick 2, looking there for his ninth trick). Looks like declarer has five club tricks, two diamonds, and the heart. If partner had the diamond king, he would have risen and played a heart to you. If declarer has Hand 1, he has a third diamond trick and you cannot set him. You needed to lead a spade. You can set Hands 2, 3 and 4, but not by the same play in each case. Against Hand 2, you need to cash the heart suit now; cashing one heart will reveal that layout. Hand 3 needs a spade shift, but most South players would pass with that emaciated holding, so you will discount that case. Hand 4 can be set by returning a club and then following declarer's discards in the four-card ending. He must either unguard the king of spades or his precious ten of hearts. You save the suit he has unguarded and pitch the other.

The real problem is in judging which hand to play for. Partner's seven of hearts at Trick 1 suggests that he started with an even number. If you cash the jack of hearts, partner will give you a present count signal that may help. Either the six or five of hearts will tell you he started with exactly two, and you will know you are defending against Hand 4. If he plays the four you are in a quandary. You cannot differentiate between an original holding of ♡74 or ♡10764, and you must make a guess!

On the actual hand, partner plays the six, and you know to base your defense on Hand 4. If declarer shows up with Hand 3, double and lead a spade next time.

The whole deal was:

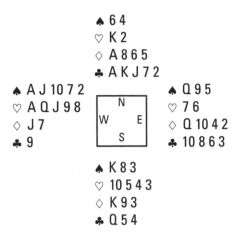

```
                    ♠ 6 4
                    ♡ K 2
                    ◇ A 8 6 5
                    ♣ A K J 7 2
  ♠ A J 10 7 2                      ♠ Q 9 5
  ♡ A Q J 9 8          N            ♡ 7 6
  ◇ J 7           W        E        ◇ Q 10 4 2
  ♣ 9                  S            ♣ 10 8 6 3
                    ♠ K 8 3
                    ♡ 10 5 4 3
                    ◇ K 9 3
                    ♣ Q 5 4
```

Note that the heart queen was a poor choice of opening leads. With a sure entry in a side suit, the ace of hearts was a much better choice. Then when you see dummy, you continue with a low heart and wait for your setting tricks.

Declarer's play could also be improved upon, since he can always make the hand after the heart queen lead. Instead of ducking a diamond, he can run all the clubs and cash the ace and king of diamonds. Now if you unguard your spade ace, he ducks a spade, and if you retain the ace and a small spade, he leads a heart from dummy. You make three heart tricks and the ace of spades, but must concede the king of spades for the game-going trick.

In the 1971 World Championship Round Robin, the declarer for the Aces (representing North America) was plus 600 against the other North American team.

```
              ♠ 8
              ♡ A 10 8
              ◇ 7 6 5 4 3
              ♣ Q 10 8 4
  ♠ 10 6
  ♡ Q 3         ┌─────────┐
  ◇ A Q 10 9    │    N    │
  ♣ K 9 6 5 3   │ W     E │
                │    S    │
                └─────────┘
```

WEST	NORTH	EAST	SOUTH
You		*Partner*	
pass	pass	pass	1♡
2NT	pass	3♣	3♠[1]
pass	4♡	all pass	

1.   Canapé, 5-5, 6-4, or 6-5 in the majors, less than 17 HCP.

You lead the ♣5 to partner's ace and declarer's jack. Partner returns the ♡2 to your queen and dummy's ace. Declarer plays the ♣Q and pitches the ◇8. You win the king and cash the ace of diamonds, dropping declarer's king. And now?

SOLUTION TO PROBLEM 26

Hand 1	Hand 2	Hand 3	Hand 4
♠ A Q J 9 7 5	♠ A K J 9 7 5	♠ A K J 9 7 5	♠ A K J 7 5
♡ K 9 7 5	♡ K 9 7 5	♡ K J 9 5	♡ K 9 7 5 4
◊ K 8	◊ K 8	◊ K 8	◊ K 8
♣ J	♣ J	♣ J	♣ J

You know declarer is 5-5 or 6-4 in the majors, but which is it? Holding six spades, as in Hands 1 and 2, declarer has no chance of finding ten tricks. With a hand like 3, he is beaten by a diamond continuation, but after partner's trump return, declarer had ten tricks by finessing the jack of spades, ruffing a spade, and drawing the remaining trumps. If partner had four trumps, he probably would have started a forcing defense by returning a diamond at Trick 2.

These assumptions lead you to Hand 4. In this case, a heart return holds declarer to five heart tricks, one club, two spades and one ruff, for a total of nine tricks. Any other play lets him score ten tricks via two ruffs in dummy, three in his hand, the ace and king of trumps, the ace and king of spades, and a club. Had declarer finessed the spade at Trick 3, he would still have been left with only nine tricks. Of course, on your heart return, partner must cover dummy's ten with the jack. Otherwise declarer has an entry to use for a spade finesse and his tenth trick.

The whole deal:

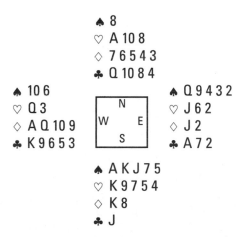

♠ 8
♡ A 10 8
◊ 7 6 5 4 3
♣ Q 10 8 4

♠ 10 6
♡ Q 3
◊ A Q 10 9
♣ K 9 6 5 3

♠ Q 9 4 3 2
♡ J 6 2
◊ J 2
♣ A 7 2

♠ A K J 7 5
♡ K 9 7 5 4
◊ K 8
♣ J

When this deal was played in the 1971 World Championship Round Robin, the declarer for the Aces was plus 420 against Australia.

PROBLEM 27

```
        ♠ 10 9 8
        ♡ Q 10
        ◇ Q 8 4 2
        ♣ Q 6 5 2
                    ♠ A J 3
        ┌─────┐     ♡ 7 2
        │  N  │     ◇ K J 10 9
        │W   E│     ♣ A 9 7 4
        │  S  │
        └─────┘
```

The bidding:

WEST	NORTH	EAST	SOUTH
Partner		*You*	
		1NT¹	2♡
dbl	all pass		

1.   12-14 HCP.

Playing standard leads, partner leads the ♣J. Dummy plays low, you play the seven, and declarer's king wins. A heart to dummy's ten wins, and declarer leads a spade from dummy. Over to you.

SOLUTION TO PROBLEM 27

Hand 1	Hand 2	Hand 3	Hand 4	Hand 5
♠ K 6 2	♠ K Q 6	♠ Q 6 2	♠ Q 6 2	♠ K Q 6
♡ K 9 6 5 4 3	♡ K 9 6 5 4 3	♡ K 9 6 5 4 3	♡ K 9 6 5 4 3	♡ K 9 6 5 4 3
◊ A 3	◊ 3	◊ A	◊ A 3	◊ 5 3
♣ K 8	♣ K 10 3	♣ K 10 3	♣ K 8	♣ K 8

Five alternatives! Remember, this is a doubled partscore, and whether you're playing IMPs or matchpoints, a great deal rides on the outcome. Opposite a weak notrump, partner needs about ten points and good hearts for his double. Hands 1 and 2 are cold for eight tricks so you hope you are defending against some other hand. You must focus on Hands 3, 4, and 5. Doubles against these hands are all borderline, but partner is a many times national champion. Declarer, however, is a world champion.

To set Hand 3, you need to take three spades, a heart, a club and a club ruff. Hand 4 goes down with three spades, a heart, a diamond and a club. Hand 5 needs a trump promotion, to go along with a spade, a heart, two diamonds and the ace of clubs. How can you sort out these possibilities?

First, you must rise with the ace of spades and look for partner's attitude signal. If he plays a high spade to indicate a spade honor, look for Hand 3 or 4 and go passive. Return a trump, and see what partner does. He will win the ace of hearts, and with a doubleton club as in Hand 3, he will return a low one, and you will give him a ruff. If he returns the ten of clubs, you play him for an initial holding of three clubs and just continue clubs as you wait for your six tricks (three spades, one heart, one club and one diamond).

Against Hand 5, partner will play a low spade and you will place declarer with ♠KQ(x) and partner with the ace of diamonds. You shift to a diamond. Partner wins, reverts to clubs, and the defense continues with a third round. When he wins the ace of hearts, partner puts you in with a diamond, and you lead the fourth club to promote the jack of hearts.

Notice that winning the ace of spades is necessary on Hand 5 and costs nothing on Hands 3 and 4. Defending against Hand 5, the duck gives declarer a tempo and allows him to revert to trumps. He can then draw partner's trumps and score eight tricks. Perish the thought that ducking the spade will induce a misguess by declarer.

The whole deal:

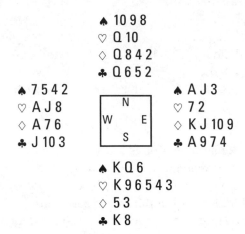

```
              ♠ 10 9 8
              ♡ Q 10
              ◇ Q 8 4 2
              ♣ Q 6 5 2
♠ 7 5 4 2                      ♠ A J 3
♡ A J 8          N             ♡ 7 2
◇ A 7 6       W     E          ◇ K J 10 9
♣ J 10 3         S            ♣ A 9 7 4
              ♠ K Q 6
              ♡ K 9 6 5 4 3
              ◇ 5 3
              ♣ K 8
```

In the 1971 World Championship Round Robin, the declarer for the Aces was plus 470 against China.

♠ K 10 7
♡ A 10 8 4
◇ K Q
♣ Q J 6 2

♠ A 5
♡ 3 2
◇ J 10 9 3
♣ A K 10 8 7

The bidding:

WEST	NORTH	EAST	SOUTH
You		*Partner*	
1◇	dbl	2◇	dbl[1]
3♣	dbl	3◇	3♡
pass	4♡	all pass	

1.   Responsive.

You lead the king of clubs, partner plays the nine, and declarer the three. Next?

SOLUTION TO PROBLEM 28

Hand 1	Hand 2	Hand 3
♠ Q J 4 2	♠ Q J 4 2	♠ Q 9 4 2
♡ K 9 7 6 5	♡ K 9 6 5	♡ K J 6 5
◇ A 8	◇ A 8	◇ A 8
♣ 5 4	♣ 5 4 3	♣ 5 4 3

If partner has the ◇A, you will have no trouble setting this, so you need to explore possibilities assuming declarer has that card. If he has Hand 1, declarer needs to guess trumps, which will not be difficult after the auction. If you are defending against Hand 2, partner's trumps are good enough to set the hand. Holding Hand 3, declarer needs to find both the queen of hearts and jack of spades, and unless you give partner a club ruff right now, declarer may do just that. A club at Trick 2 must be right, because it is now or never for a club ruff. Depending on what partner plays on your ace of clubs, you follow either with a club for partner to ruff or the jack of diamonds, hoping.

The whole deal:

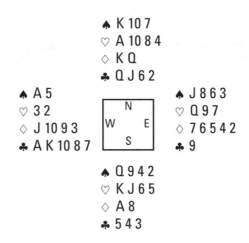

	♠ K 10 7	
	♡ A 10 8 4	
	◇ K Q	
	♣ Q J 6 2	
♠ A 5		♠ J 8 6 3
♡ 3 2	N	♡ Q 9 7
◇ J 10 9 3	W E	◇ 7 6 5 4 2
♣ A K 10 8 7	S	♣ 9
	♠ Q 9 4 2	
	♡ K J 6 5	
	◇ A 8	
	♣ 5 4 3	

```
        ♠ 7 2
        ♡ K 9 4 2
        ◇ 9 8 7 6
        ♣ 9 6 4
                    ♠ A Q J 8
        ┌─────┐     ♡ J 10 7
        │  N  │     ◇ A 10 2
        │W   E│     ♣ Q 8 2
        │  S  │
        └─────┘
```

The bidding:

WEST	NORTH	EAST	SOUTH
PARTNER		*YOU*	
		1♠	1NT
dbl	all pass		

Partner's seven of clubs goes to your queen and declarer's king. Declarer leads the king of diamonds, and partner plays the five as you win your ace. How does it look?

SOLUTION TO PROBLEM 29

Hand 1
♠ K 10 6 5
♡ A 8 3
♢ K Q J 3
♣ K 5

Hand 2
♠ K 10 6 5
♡ Q 8 3
♢ K Q J 3
♣ K 3

Hand 3
♠ 10 6 5 4
♡ A Q 3
♢ K Q J 3
♣ K 3

With five spades, declarer might have let you stew in one spade, hoping that his partner could stir the auction up; it is therefore likely that he has only four spades. That would give partner three cards in your suit, and he should have five good clubs to have decided to lead one. The vital high cards you must account for are the king of spades, the ace and queen of hearts, and the ace of clubs. Partner needs two of them for his double. If he has the ace of clubs and the queen of hearts, a marginal holding for a double (Hand 1), the hand is cold. Hand 2 is a very light 1NT overcall, but aggressive players bid that way. A spade return sets it two tricks.

The most likely layout is Hand 3, where declarer has 15 points. Your queen of spades shift will hold the trick, and then you lead a club so that partner can cash all his club tricks. He will revert to spades then, and you will defeat the hand three tricks. In the 1971 World Championship, the Aces declarer did hold Hand 3, but the contract made against North American defenders after a heart return.

The complete layout:

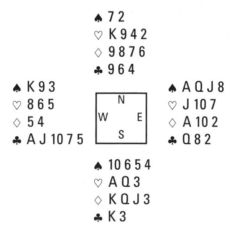

```
                    ♠ 7 2
                    ♡ K 9 4 2
                    ♢ 9 8 7 6
                    ♣ 9 6 4
    ♠ K 9 3        ┌─────────┐      ♠ A Q J 8
    ♡ 8 6 5        │    N    │      ♡ J 10 7
    ♢ 5 4        W │         │ E    ♢ A 10 2
    ♣ A J 10 7 5   │    S    │      ♣ Q 8 2
                   └─────────┘
                    ♠ 10 6 5 4
                    ♡ A Q 3
                    ♢ K Q J 3
                    ♣ K 3
```

```
              ♠ 10 9
              ♡ 8
              ◇ A K 10 9 6 3
              ♣ Q J 6 4
♠ K 6 5 3    ┌─────────┐
♡ Q 9 5      │    N    │
◇ J 8 4      │ W     E │
♣ K 8 7      │    S    │
             └─────────┘
```

The bidding, with both sides vulnerable, was:

WEST	NORTH	EAST	SOUTH
You		*Partner*	
	3◇	pass	3NT
all pass			

You lead the ♠3 to the nine, queen, and ace. Declarer continues with a low club. What do you visualize and how do you defend?

SOLUTION TO PROBLEM 30

You can bank on declarer having six diamond tricks (otherwise he would have started diamonds immediately).

Here are four possible hands:

Hand 1	Hand 2	Hand 3	Hand 4
♠ A J	♠ A J 4 2	♠ A J 4	♠ A J 4
♡ J 10 7 6 4	♡ A 10 7 6	♡ K 10 7 6	♡ K 10 7 6
◇ Q 7 5	◇ Q 7	◇ Q 7	◇ Q 7 5
♣ A 5 3	♣ 5 3 2	♣ A 5 3 2	♣ 5 3 2

If declarer has Hand 1, the defense is ready to run the spade suit as soon as you gain the lead. Declarer's best shot for nine tricks was to run six diamonds and take the club finesse. No good declarer would ever lead a low club towards dummy at Trick 2 with this hand.

With Hand 2 declarer had nine tricks by playing a spade at Trick 2. Holding Hand 3, he is going to make at least four notrump. You expect partner to have the ace of hearts and the ace of clubs, so you defend on the assumption of Hand 4. It is important that you assume captaincy of the defense at Trick 2, because you know more about the spade suit than partner does. You know that declarer has a second spade stopper and that two heart tricks are needed by the defense; partner does not. Win the ♣K and lead a heart. Partner can tell from your low heart card that you want a return of the suit. The defense thus takes two hearts, one spade, and two clubs for a one-trick set.

The whole deal:

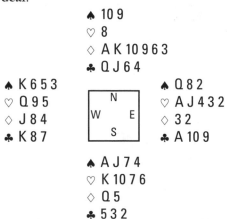

```
              ♠ 10 9
              ♡ 8
              ◇ A K 10 9 6 3
              ♣ Q J 6 4
♠ K 6 5 3          N          ♠ Q 8 2
♡ Q 9 5       W       E       ♡ A J 4 3 2
◇ J 8 4            S          ◇ 3 2
♣ K 8 7                       ♣ A 10 9
              ♠ A J 7 4
              ♡ K 10 7 6
              ◇ Q 5
              ♣ 5 3 2
```

In the 1971 World Championship Round Robin, the Australian declarer made his contract against the Aces.

♠ 9 6 4 2
♡ A K J 10
◇ K 4
♣ K J 10

♠ A 5
♡ 9 5 3
◇ A J 10
♣ Q 8 7 5 2

```
      N
   W     E
      S
```

WEST	NORTH	EAST	SOUTH
You		*Partner*	
	1NT	pass	2♣
pass	2NT[1]	pass	4♠
all pass			

1. Both majors, minimum.

You lead the ♣5 to the ten and partner's ace. Declarer ruffs and plays a diamond to dummy's king and partner's nine. He then plays a spade to partner's eight and his own queen. The winning play is…?

SOLUTION TO PROBLEM 31

Hand 1
♠ Q J 10 7 3
♡ 4 2
◇ Q 7 6 5 3 2
♣ —

Hand 2
♠ Q J 10 7 3
♡ Q 7 4 2
◇ Q 7 6 5
♣ —

Hand 3
♠ Q J 7 3
♡ Q 7 4
◇ Q 7 6 5 3 2
♣ —

Declarer chose to travel to dummy to lead the first round of spades, suggesting a broken suit, so you can rule out Hand 1. Hand 2 is also inconsistent with partner's play, because you want him to play second highest when following with a four-card holding, not highest. He must have a doubleton or singleton diamond.

These clues suggest a layout like Hand 3, which can be set by winning the ace of spades and playing the ace of diamonds and another diamond. Partner overruffs dummy and cashes the king of spades.

The whole deal:

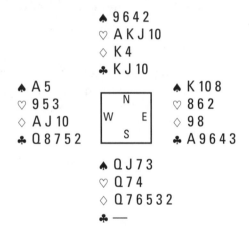

In the 1971 World Championship Round Robin, the Chinese defender ducked the spade ace, and the French declarer was plus 620.

♠ 10 9 5
♡ A
◇ A Q 4
♣ J 9 5 4 3 2

♠ 2
♡ K Q 3 2
◇ 8 7 5 2
♣ A K Q 10

North-South are vulnerable.

WEST	NORTH	EAST	SOUTH
You		*Partner*	
			2♠
dbl	4♠	5♡	pass
pass	5♠	dbl	all pass

You lead the ♣K, partner plays the six, and declarer the seven. From the look of dummy, North certainly trusts his partner's weak two-bids! How do you set this contract?

SOLUTION TO PROBLEM 32

Hand 1	Hand 2	Hand 3
♠ K Q J 6 4 3	♠ A Q J 7 6 4	♠ A Q J 7 6 4 3
♡ 9 8 7	♡ 9 8 7	♡ 9 7
◇ K 6	◇ J 6	◇ 6 3
♣ 8 7	♣ 8 7	♣ 8 7

Partner is marked with a singleton club, and you have no entry to use your club later if you do not cash it now. There are three important cards out on this deal – the ace and king of trumps, and the ◇K. Partner should have two of them for his double. For example, if declarer has Hand 1, partner has only the ♠A and two jacks, hardly enough to warrant a double. You must either shift to a trump, so that partner can play ace and another, or cash the ♣K and lead anything. A diamond shift right away would allow declarer to pitch a club and make eleven tricks.

Hand 2 is set by either a club continuation or a diamond shift. Declarer cannot set up clubs, pick up partner's Kxx of trumps, then travel to dummy to use the clubs. If he has Hand 3, a club continuation or a spade return allows declarer to make eleven tricks. He has enough entries to ruff out the clubs and pitch his losing diamond. Only a diamond shift beats this hand. Partner needs both the ◇K and ◇J, because if declarer has the ◇J along with seven spades, he can pitch his club.

There is no absolutely correct defense here: you must make a judgement. A diamond shift is more consistent with partner's likely hand for his penalty double. Without the ◇K, he has a poor double.

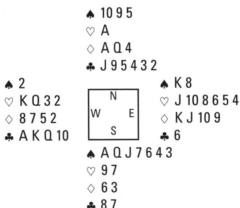

```
                    ♠ 10 9 5
                    ♡ A
                    ◇ A Q 4
                    ♣ J 9 5 4 3 2
  ♠ 2               ┌──────┐        ♠ K 8
  ♡ K Q 3 2         │  N   │        ♡ J 10 8 6 5 4
  ◇ 8 7 5 2       W │      │ E      ◇ K J 10 9
  ♣ A K Q 10        │  S   │        ♣ 6
                    └──────┘
                    ♠ A Q J 7 6 4 3
                    ♡ 9 7
                    ◇ 6 3
                    ♣ 8 7
```

In the 1971 World Championship Round Robin, the Australian declarer was plus 850 against the Aces.

♠ Q J 10 3
♡ J 9
◇ 5 4
♣ Q J 10 7 3

♠ K 4
♡ K 8 4 2
◇ 9 7 2
♣ A 9 6 2

```
    N
W       E
    S
```

WEST	NORTH	EAST	SOUTH
You		*Partner*	
			1♣¹
pass	1◇²	pass	1♠³
pass	3♠	pass	4♠
all pass			

1. Roman.
2. Negative.
3. Four spades without four hearts, balanced 12-16 HCP.

You lead the ♡2 to the jack, five, and declarer's ten. Declarer leads the ♠Q from dummy, partner follows with the five, and declarer plays the two as you win the king. You know declarer's heart and spade holdings. Can you recover from your disastrous lead?

SOLUTION TO PROBLEM 33

Hand 1	Hand 2	Hand 3	Hand 4
♠ A 9 6 2	♠ A 9 6 2	♠ A 9 6 2	♠ A 9 6 2
♡ A Q 10	♡ A Q 10	♡ A Q 10	♡ A Q 10
◇ K 8	◇ K Q 8 6	◇ K 8 6	◇ A J 8 6
♣ K 8 5 4	♣ 8 4	♣ K 8 4	♣ 8 4

Hand 1 offers the defenders only one chance for a club ruff. It needs the ♣A to be played now, followed by the obvious ruff. Hand 2 is always down. Defending against Hand 3, there is also a club ruff, but the defense can survive a diamond to East's ace, and he will return his singleton club. Hand 4 demands a diamond switch before declarer's clubs are set up. Which is it?

Partner played the lowest outstanding spade, on a hand where he is known to have three trumps, so he cannot want a ruff. Try a diamond shift, and play declarer for Hand 4.

The whole deal:

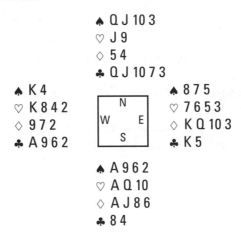

```
                ♠ Q J 10 3
                ♡ J 9
                ◇ 5 4
                ♣ Q J 10 7 3
  ♠ K 4                        ♠ 8 7 5
  ♡ K 8 4 2        N           ♡ 7 6 5 3
  ◇ 9 7 2     W       E        ◇ K Q 10 3
  ♣ A 9 6 2        S           ♣ K 5
                ♠ A 9 6 2
                ♡ A Q 10
                ◇ A J 8 6
                ♣ 8 4
```

In the 1971 World Championship Round Robin, the Brazilian declarer scored plus 620 against North America.

PROBLEM **34**

```
        ♠ 9 7
        ♡ A 9 8 4
        ◇ A K J 7 5 4
        ♣ 7
♠ 10 6 5        ┌─────────┐
♡ Q J 6 2       │    N    │
◇ 6             │ W     E │
♣ A K J 4 3     │    S    │
                └─────────┘
```

WEST	NORTH	EAST	SOUTH
You		*PARTNER*	
	1◇	pass	2♠
pass	3◇	pass	3♠
pass	4♡	pass	4♠
pass	5♣	pass	5◇
pass	6◇	pass	6♠
all pass			

You lead the ♡2 to the four, seven, and declarer's ten. Declarer leads the ♣5 to your jack, dummy's seven, and partner's two. And now?

SOLUTION TO PROBLEM 34

Hand 1	Hand 2	Hand 3	Hand 4
♠ A K Q J 4 3 2	♠ A K Q J 4 2	♠ A K Q J 4 2	♠ A K Q J 4 2
♡ K 10	♡ K 10	♡ K 10 5	♡ K 10
◇ 2	◇ 3 2	◇ 2	◇ 2
♣ Q 8 6	♣ Q 8 6	♣ Q 8 6	♣ Q 8 6 5

Hand 1 was cold after your brilliant lead. Declarer could simply draw trumps, unblock the king of hearts, and cash dummy's high red cards. Hands 2 and 3 have sufficient communication that declarer can ruff a club and always cash his red-suit cards. Hand 4 is your target. A diamond now will kill declarer's communications; he can neither ruff two clubs nor ruff one and cash four red-suit tricks.

Would you (as West) have led the ace of clubs, and shifted to a trump? At the other table, the defense tried that, and declarer found the squeeze in hearts and clubs. A diamond shift would also have beaten the hand after a club lead.

The whole deal:

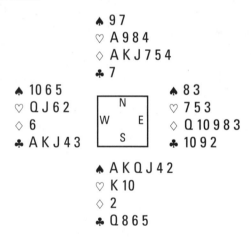

In the 1971 World Championship Round Robin, the impossible slam made at both tables!

♠ A 10 6 5
♡ 8 7 3
◇ K Q J 3 2
♣ 8

♠ K J 9 8 7 2
♡ J 9 6
◇ 8 7
♣ A 5

WEST	NORTH	EAST	SOUTH
You		*Partner*	
			1♣
2♠	2NT	pass	3♠
pass	5◇	pass	6♣
all pass			

You lead a small spade to dummy's five and partner's queen. Declarer ruffs with the ♣2. Declarer next leads the king of clubs and you win your ace. What now?

SOLUTION TO PROBLEM 35

Declarer has a solid hand. He was never planning to play in diamonds, and his cuebid was based on a long, one-loser club suit in addition to a good heart holding. If declarer has both the red-suit aces, the defense has no hope. If you are going to set declarer, he must have bid a slam off two aces, and you must guess which ace partner holds. Here are a couple of South hands to consider.

Hand 1   ♠ — ♡ A K Q 2 ◇ 4 ♣ K Q J 10 9 6 4 2

Hand 2   ♠ — ♡ K Q 4 2 ◇ A 10 ♣ K Q J 9 6 4 2

Defending against Hand 1, a diamond return is the only way to set the hand. But with that hand, declarer would have pitched his diamond loser at Trick 1 and waltzed home with his slam. Whenever declarer has two small diamonds, one pitch will not help, and he will always have a diamond loser.

Turn your attention to Hand 2. You must lead a heart to set this hand. A diamond return allows declarer to win, draw trumps, and pitch three hearts on the diamonds and one on the ace of spades.

The diamond ace will not go away but the heart ace might. You must play a heart now.

The actual layout was:

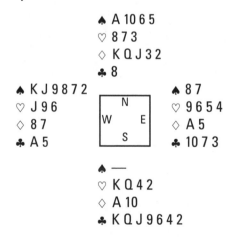

```
                    ♠ A 10 6 5
                    ♡ 8 7 3
                    ◇ K Q J 3 2
                    ♣ 8
   ♠ K J 9 8 7 2          ┌─────┐          ♠ 8 7
   ♡ J 9 6                │  N  │          ♡ 9 6 5 4
   ◇ 8 7                  │W   E│          ◇ A 5
   ♣ A 5                  │  S  │          ♣ 10 7 3
                          └─────┘
                    ♠ —
                    ♡ K Q 4 2
                    ◇ A 10
                    ♣ K Q J 9 6 4 2
```

In the 1979 World Championship round robin, the American declarer made his impossible slam when the Brazilian defender returned a diamond after winning the ace of clubs

♠ K 5 4
♡ K J 9 5
◇ A 9 8 3 2
♣ 9

♠ A Q 2
♡ 10 2
◇ Q 7
♣ A K Q 8 7 4

```
        N
    W       E
        S
```

WEST	NORTH	EAST	SOUTH
You		*Partner*	
1♣	dbl	pass	4♠
all pass			

You lead the ♣K, and partner and declarer both follow with low cards. You continue with the queen, showing that you have an odd number of clubs remaining. Declarer ruffs low in dummy and partner plays the jack.

Declarer then leads a heart to partner's eight and his ace, and plays the seven of spades. How do you proceed?

SOLUTION TO PROBLEM 36

Declarer has some number of spades to the jack or ten, the ace of hearts, and, no doubt, the king of diamonds. Partner's carding shows three clubs, so declarer has three as well. Partner has an even number of hearts, four or six. There are still many unknowns on this hand, and you must consider several possibilities.

Hand 1	**Hand 2**	**Hand 3**	**Hand 4**	**Hand 5**
♠ J 10 9 8 7 3	♠ J 10 9 8 7 3	♠ J 10 9 7 3	♠ 10 9 8 7 3	♠ J 10 8 7
♡ A Q 6	♡ A	♡ A Q 6	♡ A	♡ A
◇ 4	◇ K 10 9	◇ K 9	◇ K J 6 5	◇ K J 10 6 5
♣ 10 3 2	♣ 10 3 2	♣ 10 3 2	♣ 10 3 2	♣ 10 3 2

You really expect declarer to hold five or six spades for the precipitate jump to game, but no law says he has to. Hands 1, 2, and 3 all produce an easy ten tricks via two club ruffs in dummy and drawing trumps. Declarer is not doing that. He is trying to draw trumps instead of ruffing losers so you decide to focus on Hands 4 and 5. You win the ♠A, dummy plays low and partner follows with the ♠6.

Against either Hand 4 or Hand 5, a third round of clubs cannot hurt. Declarer must ruff with the ♠K. He crosses to the ◇K as partner follows with the four, and leads the ♠10. You are at the crossroads. The position now (at Trick 7) is one of the following:

Hand 4

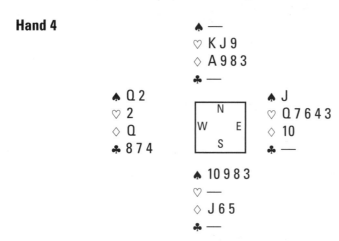

Hand 5

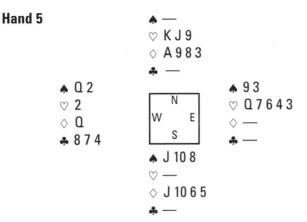

```
                    ♠ —
                    ♡ K J 9
                    ◇ A 9 8 3
                    ♣ —
  ♠ Q 2                          ♠ 9 3
  ♡ 2          N                 ♡ Q 7 6 4 3
  ◇ Q      W       E             ◇ —
  ♣ 8 7 4      S                 ♣ —
                    ♠ J 10 8
                    ♡ —
                    ◇ J 10 6 5
                    ♣ —
```

Defending Hand 4, if you rise with the queen of spades, declarer is home. Defending Hand 5, if you duck your queen of spades, declarer lands his contract. Which is it? Rise or duck? You ask two questions. Where is the ♠3? And where is the ◇10? Partner may have started a trump echo to show that he has three trumps and wants to ruff something. With the ◇10-4 originally, he would have played the ten to show a doubleton when declarer led a diamond from dummy. The clues point to Hand 5, so you must rise with the ♠Q and lead a diamond.

Note that with Hand 4, declarer could have made his contract by playing for 2-2 diamonds and using that suit for transportation, first unblocking the ace of hearts, then coming to dummy to pitch a club on the king of hearts, and crossing again to his hand to lead a trump to the king. He needs 2-2 diamonds in any case to make the hand.

The whole deal:

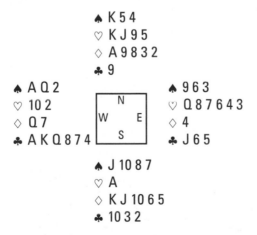

```
                    ♠ K 5 4
                    ♡ K J 9 5
                    ◇ A 9 8 3 2
                    ♣ 9
  ♠ A Q 2                        ♠ 9 6 3
  ♡ 10 2           N             ♡ Q 8 7 6 4 3
  ◇ Q 7        W       E         ◇ 4
  ♣ A K Q 8 7 4    S             ♣ J 6 5
                    ♠ J 10 8 7
                    ♡ A
                    ◇ K J 10 6 5
                    ♣ 10 3 2
```

In the 1971 World Championship Round Robin in the match between France and Brazil, the play of rising with the ace of spades and playing a third round of clubs was not found, and declarer made his contract.

♠ K J 6 3
♡ 10 9 7 2
◇ —
♣ A 10 7 6 5

♠ 8 2
♡ A K 5 4
◇ Q 4 3 2
♣ K 9 4

```
      N
  W       E
      S
```

WEST	NORTH	EAST	SOUTH
You		*Partner*	
			1NT
pass	2♣	pass	2♡[1]
pass	4♡	all pass	

1.   16-17 HCP, balanced, four hearts.

You lead the ◇ 2, ruffed in dummy, as partner plays the five and declarer the six. Declarer plays dummy's ♡ 10, partner plays the eight, declarer follows with the three and you duck. Declarer plays the ♠ 3 to partner's five and his ace. He ruffs the eight of diamonds in dummy as partner plays the seven. Declarer then leads the ♡ 9 from dummy as partner pitches the ◇ 9. You win and…?

SOLUTION TO PROBLEM 37

The diamond situation should be known to both defenders. Declarer's decision to ruff the opening lead in dummy is revealing. With AKJ, AK109, AJ10x, or a similar holding, he would run the opening lead to his hand. He could then either win a free finesse or later take a ruffing finesse through you. The fact that he ruffed the lead shows that he has no tenace and no useful spot cards. Therefore, declarer's heart and diamond holdings are known, and the hand reduces to two possibilities.

Hand 1	Hand 2
♠ A Q 4	♠ A 10 4
♡ Q J 6 3	♡ Q J 6 3
◇ A K 8 6	◇ A K 8 6
♣ 8 3	♣ Q 8

You can set Hand 1 by returning a club and Hand 2 by returning a spade. Which is it? Holding Hand 2, declarer might have gone after the club suit for his tricks. Catching one club honor in your hand would let him make his game. A second clue can be found in partner's spot card plays. If he holds a concentration in one suit, especially with no other high cards in his hand, he should be trying to signal suit preference. With, say, QJx in clubs (the lowest ranking side suit) he should play the smallest cards possible every time he follows suit or discards. Finally, declarer risked having the defense draw trumps after only one diamond ruff. He could afford that with Hand 1 where he would end up with ten ready-made tricks, but not Hand 2.

The clues all point to Hand 1. A club lead now positions you to ruff the third spade (and cash the king of clubs) if declarer tries for a club pitch. If he tries to draw trumps, you win and play king and another club. The third club forces declarer and sets up your fourth trump for the setting trick.

The whole deal:

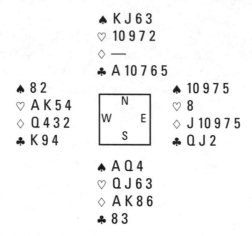

```
                    ♠ K J 6 3
                    ♡ 10 9 7 2
                    ◇ —
                    ♣ A 10 7 6 5
    ♠ 8 2                          ♠ 10 9 7 5
    ♡ A K 5 4         N            ♡ 8
    ◇ Q 4 3 2    W         E       ◇ J 10 9 7 5
    ♣ K 9 4           S            ♣ Q J 2
                    ♠ A Q 4
                    ♡ Q J 6 3
                    ◇ A K 8 6
                    ♣ 8 3
```

In the 1971 World Championship final against France, the Aces scored plus 650 on this deal.

♠ J 8 7 4
♡ A 7 6 3
◇ K 9 8 6
♣ 9

♠ K 3
♡ J 10 4
◇ J 7
♣ A K J 10 7 3

```
  N
W   E
  S
```

The following auction takes place.

WEST	NORTH	EAST	SOUTH
You		*Partner*	
		pass	1NT
pass	2♣	pass	2♡
pass	4♡	all pass	

You lead the king of clubs, partner playing the six and declarer the four. Now what?

SOLUTION TO PROBLEM 38

You have very little to go on here. It is only Trick 2, and you must make important decisions. The jack of diamonds looks useful, if only partner has the queen. If partner has the ace of diamonds, declarer may misguess and lose two diamonds. Your heart holding is potentially useful. Maybe partner has the queen. Both red queens would be perfect. Of course, every declarer in the world would go down then. If partner has the ace of spades, you can set the hand right now by getting a ruff. What to do?

Hand 1	Hand 2	Hand 3
♠ A Q 10 9	♠ A Q 10 9	♠ Q 10 9
♡ K 9 8 6	♡ K Q 9 8	♡ K Q 9 8
◇ A 10 5	◇ Q 10 5	◇ A Q 5 4
♣ Q 4	♣ Q 4	♣ Q 4

Defending Hand 1, a passive (forcing) defense works. Declarer must lose a trick in each suit. Against Hand 2, you must hope for two diamond tricks. Defending Hand 3, you can get a spade ruff.

But wait! Against Hand 3, you also prevail by continuing a club. Declarer ruffs in dummy, but he needs one spade trick for his contract. He has only nine tricks otherwise. If he draws trump and leads a spade, you force him in his hand. Now he is out of trumps. When he plays a second round of spades, the defense comes to a club trick. If he draws only two rounds of trumps and plays spades, you get your ruff.

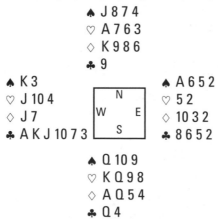

                    ♠ J 8 7 4
                    ♡ A 7 6 3
                    ◇ K 9 8 6
                    ♣ 9
    ♠ K 3   ♠ A 6 5 2
    ♡ J 10 4   N   ♡ 5 2
    ◇ J 7   W   E   ◇ 10 3 2
    ♣ A K J 10 7 3   S   ♣ 8 6 5 2
                    ♠ Q 10 9
                    ♡ K Q 9 8
                    ◇ A Q 5 4
                    ♣ Q 4

In the 1979 World Championship round robin, four hearts was the contract four times. Italy's Benito Garozzo was the only defender to prevail. The contract made at three tables when the West defender switched to a trump at Trick 2. Eisenberg also found the defense, but he was defending three hearts.

♠ A Q x
♡ x x x
◇ x
♣ K 10 x x x x

```
        N
    W       E
        S
```

♠ x
♡ A Q 9 8 7
◇ K Q J x x
♣ x x

WEST	NORTH	EAST	SOUTH
Partner		*You*	
		1♡	1♠
dbl	2♣	2◇	pass
pass	2♠	3◇	pass
pass	3♠	pass	pass
dbl	all pass		

Partner leads the ten of hearts, and although it is only Trick 1, you are already at the point where your play will determine the outcome of the hand.

You expect partner to have four spades for his double of 3♠, along with four clubs and four diamonds for his original negative double of 1♠. He should also have two aces. These are all likelihoods but not certainties.

SOLUTION TO PROBLEM 39

You have shown a distributional hand and yet partner has chosen to make a penalty double of a partscore. You expect the opponents to play this hand in three diamonds at the other table, and they will be plus 110 with your cards. At your table, you might have set three spades undoubled one or two tricks for plus 50 or perhaps plus 100. Partner expects to gain either 2 IMPs or 5 IMPs by doubling, versus losing 12 IMPs if the opponents make their contract. He needs to be very confident of a set (odds of three or four to one) to justify his double.

You still don't like it. Perspiration decorates your brow as you mentally construct five hands that bracket the possibilities suggested by the bidding.

Hand 1	Hand 2	Hand 3	Hand 4	Hand 5
♠ K J x x x	♠ J x x x x	♠ K J x x x	♠ K J x x x	♠ K 10 x x
♡ K J x	♡ K J x	♡ K J x x	♡ K J x x	♡ K J x x
♢ x x x	♢ x x x x	♢ x x x	♢ x x x	♢ x x x x
♣ x x	♣ A	♣ A	♣ Q	♣ A

Against Hand 1, you must duck the first heart. The defense must maneuver a heart ruff and two trump leads to set the hand. Against Hand 2, you must win the ace of hearts and return a trump. Hand 3 is cold against any defense.

Hand 4 goes down two if you win the ace of hearts and give partner a ruff; he returns a diamond and then you give him a second ruff. He then leads trumps twice: once when in with the second ruff, and a second time when he wins the club ace. Now declarer can do no better than take seven tricks. This is the hand you really expect for a partscore double: a singleton in your suit, and aces on the side.

Hand 5 goes down one with two heart ruffs, followed by a trump lead.

You mop your brow and play ace and another heart. You decide that the most compelling reason for partner to double a partscore at IMPs is possession of a singleton heart.

The actual hand was Hand 5, and an Austrian declarer made his contract for a 12-IMP gain against the USA in the 1985 World Championship final. The defender with your hand ducked the opening heart lead and had to concede minus 530.

The whole deal:

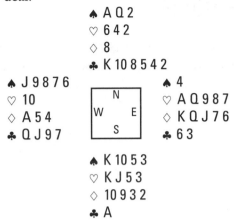

♠ A Q 2
♥ 6 4 2
♦ 8
♣ K 10 8 5 4 2

♠ J 9 8 7 6
♥ 10
♦ A 5 4
♣ Q J 9 7

♠ 4
♥ A Q 9 8 7
♦ K Q J 7 6
♣ 6 3

♠ K 10 5 3
♥ K J 5 3
♦ 10 9 3 2
♣ A

P R O B L E M 40

♠ K Q 7 5 4
♥ K 7 4 2
♦ Q J
♣ 4 3

♠ 8
♥ A Q 9 3
♦ 8 7 3 2
♣ 9 8 7 2

WEST	NORTH	EAST	SOUTH
You		*Partner*	
pass	2♦[1]	pass	2NT[2]
pass	3♦[3]	pass	4♥
all pass			

1. Five spades, four hearts, 9-14 HCP.
2. Asks about shape and strength.
3. 5-4-2-2 minimum.

You lead the nine of clubs to partner's ten and declarer's king. Declarer continues with the jack of hearts, you cover with the queen, declarer wins in dummy and leads another heart. Partner follows low and declarer plays the eight. You win the nine, and… what next?

SOLUTION TO PROBLEM 40

Why has declarer bypassed 3NT to play 4♡ knowing that he was only in a 4-3 fit and that his partner has five spades? He has two spades at most, for one thing. He must also have a weak (as in wide open) minor. The wide open minor can only be diamonds.

Hand 1	Hand 2
♠ A x	♠ A x
♡ J 10 8	♡ J 10 8
◊ K x x	◊ x x
♣ A K Q x x	♣ A K Q J x x

Two hands bracket the possibilities you need to consider. If declarer had anything like Hand 1 with strength in diamonds as well as clubs, he would have tried 3NT instead of risking 4♡ on a 4-3 fit. He surely has a holding such as Hand 2, with one minor wide open and fast tricks available once trumps are dealt with. A diamond return sets this hand three tricks.

The whole deal:

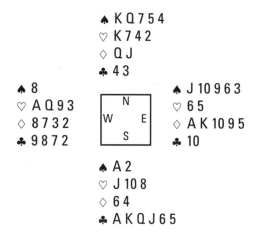

```
                      ♠ K Q 7 5 4
                      ♡ K 7 4 2
                      ◊ Q J
                      ♣ 4 3
        ♠ 8                             ♠ J 10 9 6 3
        ♡ A Q 9 3          N            ♡ 6 5
        ◊ 8 7 3 2      W       E        ◊ A K 10 9 5
        ♣ 9 8 7 2          S            ♣ 10
                      ♠ A 2
                      ♡ J 10 8
                      ◊ 6 4
                      ♣ A K Q J 6 5
```

In the 1985 World Championship final against USA, the Austrian declarer scored plus 650 when West continued clubs after winning the heart nine.

A Final Thought

"...Bright spirit of immortal Hoyle
By whose enlightened efforts Whist became
A sober, serious, scientific game;
To whose unwearied pains, while here below,
The great, th' important privilege we owe,
That random strokes disgrace our play no more
But skill presides, where all was chance before."

Alexander Thompson, in his Epic poem, **Whist**, written in 1791.
Hoyle died in 1769, aged 97.

More Bridge Titles from Master Point Press

ABTA Book of the Year Award winners

25 Bridge Conventions You Should Know
by Barbara Seagram and Marc Smith (foreword by Eddie Kantar)
192pp., PB   Can $19.95   US$ 15.95

Eddie Kantar teaches Modern Bridge Defense
Eddie Kantar teaches Advanced Bridge Defense
by Eddie Kantar
each 240pp., PB   Can $27.95   US$ 19.95

Also available in Interactive CD-ROM Editions

Modern Bridge Defense   Can $69.95, US$ 49.95
Advanced Bridge Defense Can $69.95, US$ 49.95

The Bridge Technique Series
by David Bird & Marc Smith
each 64pp. PB, Can $7.95 US $5.95

Entry Management
Safety Plays
Tricks with Trumps

Eliminations and Throw Ins
Deceptive Card Play
Planning in Suit Contracts

Reading the Cards
Tricks with Finesses
Planning in Defense

Planning in Notrump Contracts
Defensive Signaling
Squeezes for Everyone

Around the World in 80 Hands by Zia Mahmood with David Burn
256pp., PB Can $22.95 US $16.95

A Study in Silver *A second collection of bridge stories*
by David Silver
128pp., PB Can $12.95 US$ 9.95

Becoming a Bridge Expert by Frank Stewart
300pp., PB Can $27.95 US $19.95

Bridge Problems for a New Millennium by Julian Pottage
160pp., PB Can $14.95 US $14.95

Bridge the Silver Way by David Silver and Tim Bourke
192pp., PB Can $19.95 US $14.95

Bridge: 25 Ways to Compete in the Bidding.
by Barbara Seagram and Marc Smith
220pp., PB Can.$19.95 US $15.95

Bridge, Zia... and me by Michael Rosenberg
(foreword by Zia Mahmood)
192pp., PB Can $19.95 US $15.95

Challenge Your Declarer Play by Danny Roth
128pp., PB Can. $12.95 US $ 9.95

Classic Kantar a *collection of bridge humor* by Eddie Kantar
192pp., PB Can $19.95 US $14.95

Competitive Bidding in the 21st Century by Marshall Miles
254pp.,PB Can. $22.95 US. $16.95

Countdown to Winning Bridge by Tim Bourke and Marc Smith
92pp., PB Can $19.95 US $14.95

Easier Done Than Said *Brilliancy at the Bridge Table*
by Prakash K. Paranjape
128pp., PB Can $15.95 US $12.95

For Love or Money *The Life of a Bridge Journalist*
by Mark Horton and Brian Senior
189pp., PB Can $22.95 US $16.95

Focus On Declarer Play by Danny Roth
128pp., PB Can $12.95 US $9.95

Focus On Defence by Danny Roth
128pp., PB Can $12.95 US $9.95

Focus On Bidding by Danny Roth
160pp., PB   Can $14.95   US $11.95
I Shot my Bridge Partner by Matthew Granovetter
384pp., PB   Can $19.95   US $14.95

Murder at the Bridge Table by Matthew Granovetter
320pp., PB   Can $19.95   US $14.95

Partnership Bidding a w*orkbook* by Mary Paul
96pp., PB   Can $9.95   US $7.95

Playing with the Bridge Legends by Barnet Shenkin
(forewords by Zia and Michael Rosenberg)
240pp., PB   Can $24.95   US $17.95

Saints and Sinners *The St. Titus Bridge Challenge*
by David Bird & Tim Bourke
192pp., PB   Can $19.95   US $14.95

Samurai Bridge *A tale of old Japan* by Robert F. MacKinnon
256pp., PB   Can $ 22.95   US $16.95

Tales out of School *'Bridge 101' and other stories* by David Silver
(foreword by Dorothy Hayden Truscott)
128pp., PB   Can $ 12.95   US $9.95

The Bridge Magicians by Mark Horton and Radoslaw Kielbasinski
248pp., PB   Can $24.95   US $17.95

The Bridge Player's Bedside Book edited by Tony Forrester
256pp., HC   Can $27.95   US $19.95

The Complete Book of BOLS Bridge Tips edited by Sally Brock
176pp., PB (photographs)   Can $24.95   US$17.95

There Must Be A Way... *52 challenging bridge hands*
by Andrew Diosy (foreword by Eddie Kantar)
96pp., PB $9.95 US & Can.

You Have to See This... *52 more challenging bridge problems*
by Andrew Diosy and Linda Lee
96pp., PB   Can $12.95   US $9.95

Win the Bermuda Bowl with me by Jeff Meckstsroth and Marc Smith
188pp., PB   Can $24.95   US $17.95

World Class — *conversations with the bridge masters*
by Marc Smith
288pp., PB (photographs)   Can $24.95   US $17.95